Books by Raymond Lamont Brown

A BOOK OF EPITAPHS

A BOOK OF PROVERBS

A BOOK OF SUPERSTITIONS

A BOOK OF WITCHCRAFT

PHANTOMS OF THE SEA

PHANTOMS OF THE SEA

legends, customs and superstitions

RAYMOND LAMONT BROWN

Taplinger Publishing Company | New York

First published in the United States in 1973 by
TAPLINGER PUBLISHING CO., INC.
New York, New York

Library of Congress Catalog Card Number: 72-11939

ISBN 0-8008-6290-2

Second Printing

Dedicated to the memory of the German composer
RICHARD WAGNER 1813-83
whose mss and theatre bills of *Der fliegende Holländer*
in the Bibliothek of the Tribschenhaus Wagner Museum,
Lucerne, Switzerland, first inspired me
to investigate sea phantoms.

Stories of sea phantoms are innumerable and their number grows every year. Today the materialist believes that sea phantoms are a product of hallucination. Yet whether it is the phantom Viking who walks the Goodwin Sands, or the screaming sailor of Glamorgan, or even the ghostly clippers which fly before the wind off New England, all have been seen by scientifically and critically minded people and are too well attested to be lightly dismissed.

From the hundreds of authenticated ghostly sightings at sea, the most curious, famous and intriguing have been chosen for this book; they range from the celebrated *Flying Dutchman* to the ghosts aboard modern submarines. The book further traces sea occultism from early times and records some of the most fascinating superstitions concerning the sea along with its omens, monsters, customs and taboos.

Talisman drawings by Tony Raymond

Contents

Introduction	9
The *Flying Dutchman*	17
The Kaiser's Haunted Submarine	25
The Case of the Phantom Killer	32
American Sea Phantoms	40
The Case of the Headless Sailor	40
A New Haven Apparition	42
Yachtsmen's Sightings	43
The Missing River Boat	47
A Phantom Patrol	48
The Master of *The Wilmington Star*	48
Some Phantom Ships of Florida	52
A Triptych of Doomed Ships	58
Some Ghosts of the Pacific	61
The Mystery of the *Asiatic Prince*	61
The Five-masted *Copenhagen*	65
Ghost Ships of the Goodwin Sands	69
November 1753	70
The Loss of the *Violet*	72
The Wreck of the *Lady Luvibond*	73
The Mystery of the *Affray*	76
Voices from the Sea	80
Yorkshire Jack	80
The Light on Eilean Mor	83
The Cries of Pollacharra	87
The Troubled Souls of Glamorgan	88
The Haunted Isle of Scarba	95
The Somerset Sea Morgan	96
The Omen Tongues of Bells	97
Dead Sailors Walk the Shore	99
The Phantom Prowler of Canvey Point	99

The Limping Sailor of Chatham 99
The Beautiful Woman of Horning 100
The Sailor Monks of Beaulieu Abbey 101
The Ballyheigue Castle Mystery 102
The Welsh Sea Captain 104
The Phantom Intruder 105
Smuggler's Leap 106
At the Moment of Death 114
The Grey Lady of Great Isaac 116
The Ghostly Victorian Seafarer 119

Leaves from a Ghosthunter's Notebook 121
Phantoms of St Ives Bay 121
Port Danger 121
The Ghost in York Cathedral 122
A Uist Spectre Ship 125
Hoodoo aboard the *Great Eastern* 125
Saga of the *Scharnhorst* 129
Captain Alldridge's Tale 130
Ghost Pictures in the Sea 133
The Phantom Landing Craft 134
Drake's Drum 134

Occult Supplement on The British Royal Navy 136

The Occult Way of the Sea 141
The Fleets set Sail 141
Mythology and the Sea 143
Sailors' Superstitions 155
The 'Ship Wrecker' 161
Some Modern Uses of Traditional Superstitions 174
The Religious Approach 176
A Cult of Sea Monsters 179
Unscrupulous Use of Marine Occultism 184
The Ultimate Portent of Evil 185

Selected Bibliography 187

Index 189

Introduction

Ghosts do exist: of this I have no doubt. My files are too full of authenticated documents and photographs to allow me to believe anything to the contrary. Enough proof indeed to support the assertions of the late Sir Oliver Lodge, who averred: 'I tell you with all the strength of conviction which I can muster that we do persist . . . I say it on distinct scientific grounds. I say it because I know that certain friends of mine who have died exist, because I have talked with them'.

A belief in ghosts means to many an unequivocal acceptance of the souls of the dead in flowing shrouds and rusty chains, creaking and mumbling around ruined gothic mansions. This caricature has of course grown from cheap horror stories and films, no less comic strips and cabaret acts; yet it remains current in spite of the impressive number of people who continually see much less melodramatic phantoms.

Not long ago, for instance, a family in the Batley Carr area of Dewsbury, Yorkshire, England, were rehoused by the local authority because of the effect on their health of strange ghostly happenings in their council house. Council officials, police and psychics investigated the phenomena but found nothing; yet no one seemed to mock the ghostly occurrences. Eventually, a Roman Catholic priest exorcised the house and the whole proceedings were credibly reported by such papers as the *Daily Express* and the *Guardian*, all without any of the contempt which newspapers once reserved for such stories.

Actually proving that ghosts exist is quite a different matter; and should I be able to do this, with practical demonstrations of instant spectres, I would undoubtedly become a millionaire overnight. For editors, film makers, faith healers, television producers and all kinds of showmen would knock at my door with their chequebooks, eager to spend on the world's most spectacular show.

Anyone attempting to prove the case of the existence of ghosts, however, whether on land, or sea, or in the air, is setting an almost impossible task. For he or she must try to present the unseen in terms of the seen, using man's inadequate brain. The whole task is like a primitive man of 500,000 BC trying to build a spaceship of AD 2072 vintage, when he doesn't even know what a spaceship is! What is more, the ordinary man expects a simple, straightforward and easily understood proof of the existence of every ghost. This of course cannot be done, for each ghost is a law unto itself, and uses materialisation and dematerialisation techniques which are difficult for the ordinary person to comprehend.

One of the main difficulties in proving the existence of ghosts is undoubtedly the red-herrings offered by religion: even though such biblical texts as the whole of Chapter 15 of *St Paul's First Epistle to the Corinthians* remains, perhaps, the most perfect demonstration of survival of physical death in existence. While the Holy Bible presents man with a veiled answer to every question he is likely to ask concerning his existence, the interpretation of the scriptures by the prophets and chroniclers has led to many misconceptions and misunderstandings. Take for instance this quote from *Matthew XIV*, 25: 'And in the fourth watch of the night Jesus went unto them, walking on the sea'. How on earth did Jesus do it, scholars have asked for countless centuries? If they had not been blinded by the scientific rejection of the supernatural they might have assessed the incident using the various verified laws of vibration. Jesus, who was described as 'the greatest spiritualist medium ever to exist' by such researchers as the late Lord Balfour, knew exactly how to control the vibrations of the particles which made up his body. Thus he was able to cause his body to vibrate at exactly the same rate as the particles of sea water, and was therefore able to walk on the sea. An expertise known, of course, to all ghosts, and one of the supernatural powers promised to all believers by such texts as *The Revelation of St John the Divine*.

The belief in ghosts arises out of, and is a response to, some basic and universal religious human need: that of some assurance of survival after death. Both in history and pre-history ghosts have been an integral part of religious belief. Even the most primitive of religions carried the promise of immortality, inviting the belief that the spirits of the dead had to be given some sort of consideration in daily life. Naturally enough the ghosts of the communities' ancestors were the most prevalent.

Thus, ancestor worship can be offered as the first form of supernatural-religious awareness which developed in man. We know that the cave dwellers of the early Stone Age buried their dead with some ceremony, which promoted a belief in an afterlife. So, from man's early existence on earth he has *wanted* to believe in ghosts: this in itself encouraged psychic charlatanism and a naive attitude to manifestations of the supernatural.

Ghostly phenomena come in a number of categories, and this book deals with examples related to the sea. Many accounts of ghosts, for instance, are apparitions of the living, which usually appear at some crisis in the life of the person who is seen. Spectral animals too are quite common. Most ghosts, however, are revenants (those who come back from the dead) created by some violent death in the past. Ghostly lights, smoke and 'eerie feelings' make up another prominent category of ghosts.

Whilst ghosts of such objects as various means of transport are equally common, this book details the ghostly ships of history. Spectral trains have also been seen which appear to rumble through the night on their old runs, whether the railway lines still exist or not: some even cross lakes and dams! One famous legend concerns the funeral train carrying the coffin of President Abraham Lincoln, which is said to roll along a stretch of track in New York State every April.

Some ghosts return for a purpose; maybe to reveal the identity of their murderer, or to put right some misdeed which they perpetrated in life. Ghosts in modern lore have even been said to return to seek proper burial for their cadavers. The ghost of one American farmer returned for the specific purpose of informing his heirs where he had hidden his will; another American ghost returned to claim what it felt to be rightfully its own. This was the dead wife of a thrifty New England farmer, whose husband had removed her rings before the funeral, eventually to pass them on to his next wife. But the second wife awoke in terror one night to find the apparition of her predecessor angrily pulling the rings off her fingers!

This of course, is a very cursory glance at the various categories of ghost. But exactly what are people 'seeing' when they actually encounter ghosts? Is it true that a ghostly phenomenon is nothing more than a temporary derangement of the senses? Is it true that people often 'see', in eerie surroundings (ie, houses deemed haunted), what they are expected to see? Many psychologists tend to dismiss accounts of ghosts instantly as the 'product of a disturbed mind'. But for such as Sigmund Freud and Carl Jung this explanation was not enough. Freud searched for explanations among the repressed relics of our primitive past, the ancient ghost fears of primaeval man now hidden within the unconscious mind, but sometimes moving into conscious awareness. While Jung looked for answers in his theory of the collective unconscious, the contents of which could, in Jung's view, take on an almost autonomous life of their own, being projected as seemingly outward occurrences.

American psychologist William James described ghosts as products of our own unconscious minds when they are being stimulated by other minds (hypnotism, brainwashing etc are examples of mental intrusion), the telepathic contents of which he says, produce an 'objective' hallucination. F. W. H. Myers had a parallel opinion that these other minds did not stimulate captive minds directly, but by crosscurrents of thought a subject could be made to believe in hallucinatory apparitions, particularly under the influence of drugs. Yet another great British researcher of the paranormal, G. N. M. Tyrrell, late President of the Society of Psychical Research, in his *Apparitions*, proffered the theory that other minds could telepathically affect the sensory apparatus of the percipient, so that a brain received the message that a ghost was present.

All these opinions, and many more, are based on the presumption that apparitions are hallucinations. These opinions, of course, are not flexible enough and are hidebound by the inhibitions of academic cloisters which have always tended to produce gauche theories instead of positive explanations. Thus, none of the speculations we have today concerning ghosts are wholly satisfactory, and we shall never really understand ghosts until we know exactly what happens at death: this being of course, the only satisfactory revelation.

Nevertheless, the work of such as Sir William Barrett, Sir William Crookes, Professor Larkin (former astronomer of the Lowe Observatory, California), Dr Zollner, the German scientist, and the Italian researchers Professors Bozzano and Pierioni tells us much about the realm of ghosts. Pierioni, in fact, left detailed letters and journals concerning his studies of the spirit world where mediums and trance subjects had confirmed for him that 'men and women went on living after death in a country in which there were trees and houses, lakes and mountains, churches and schools'.

Because of his muscles, blood, nerves and so on the average man thinks of himself as a 'body', without which he is unable to live. What he does not realise, and what such scientists as Dr Robin J. Tillyard and Baron Schrenck-

Notzing have been proving for the past 30 years, is that he also has a gaseous etheric body which can assume a more solid form by materialisation. This solid is called ectoplasm and has been collected and examined under controlled conditions by eminent scientists like Dr W. J. Crawford of Belfast University. Ectoplasm can vary in colour, as the experiments show, from cloudy whiteness to a dark oily texture, or appear transparent, depending upon the frequency of vibration, this being the secret of how any ghost materialises or dematerialises.

The etheric body, or ghost form, can do everything that the physical body does and more. The etheric body (which is inside the mortal body) is controlled by thought waves which govern all living matter. What happens when a ghost materialises is that it gradually and deliberately reduces the vibration rate of the spirit body, which vibrates at an immensely faster rate than our ordinary mortal flesh. It is because of this tremendous rate of vibration that ordinary humans cannot see the spirit forms which are always about us. Mediums see ghosts because their 'range' of sight is greater than that of the average person. A little experiment makes the vibration hypothesis clearer: take a thin steel rod about a yard long. Stick the rod into the ground and bend it back. The steel rod at this stage is quite visible; but let go, and instantly part of the rod disappears, because it vibrates at such a rate that it becomes invisible to the human eye. Then gradually, as its vibrations slow down, it comes back into view.

Accounts of the realm of ghosts, or the afterlife, vary widely in content from medium to medium, but each one tends to follow the idea set out in *John XIV*, 2: 'In my Father's house there are many mansions'. The theories of the late Revd Arthur Ford confirmed this conception. Ford was America's foremost psychic medium, and had a list of clients ranging from Sir Arthur Conan Doyle to Bishop James A. Pike, who used him in their efforts to communicate with their dead. What might be called a 'report from the Realm of Ghosts', purporting to be written at Ford's dictation (or, as spiritualists prefer, through 'automatic writing') after his death, was produced by Ruth Montgomery and was published in 1971 as *A World Beyond* (Coward, McCann & Geoghagan). This paper gives the most recently published view of the afterlife.

According to the Ford-Montgomery notation, the newly dead who have the hardest time adjusting to their 'astral' existence are those who never believed in an afterlife; and, by inference, those who 'passed over' in traumatic circumstances, or who still have 'something earthly on their minds'. Normally, said Ford, new arrivals 'on the other side' find themselves deposited on a grassy plain replete with perfectly formed flowers and fish-filled streams. The first concern of these souls, however, is not the compatibility of their surroundings, but for their bereaved families. Only when they find that they cannot communicate with the living do most spirits realise that they have died; some never do and go on 'haunting the mortal plane'. Such may be the case with many sea phantoms.

In assessing sea phantoms an initial word or two must be said to explain the 'sea mirage' and to dissociate this from the true ghostly sighting. Mirage is the name given to various phenomena caused by reflection and refraction (bending) of light in unusual states of the atmosphere; the commonest 'state', and the most striking, is to be found in regions of calm subjected to great heat or cold (ie, hot and cold deserts and polar regions). Generally speaking, two strata of different densities lying steadily, one over the other, give rise to two images, one direct and usual, and the other an inverted reflection from the surface of contact. Thus, clouds may be reflected from a thin stratum of dense air on the sand of deserts at sunset and after, giving the appearance of water; the conventional currents of air giving a shimmering or wavy appearance, thus adding to the illusion.

At sea the layer of air on the water may in calm weather remain warmer for some height, giving an inverted reflection from above of ships below the horizon. In the early morning the inverted mirage occurs over deserts, while a shimmering image is seen at sea. It is quite possible to find mirages over roads in England by placing the eye a few inches above the ground (eg, in calm, hot weather when the air is quivering).

Looming is a form of mirage at sea, where the object viewed appears nearer and larger, but is well below the horizon. Owing to the rays of light coming over great distances and the variation in density being gradual, they curve and the image is seen along the tangent of the ray at the eye, thus there is a visual displacement. Mirages, however, do not account for many ghostly sightings at sea.

The following are the most famous of all sea phantoms. To these I have added a postscript on occult legends and superstitions of the sea, for over the centuries these have added greatly to the general mystique of the sea.

Chapter 1

The Flying Dutchman

A mong the most famous and enduring stories of phantom ships sailing the high seas is that of the *Flying Dutchman*, the spectre ship, supposed by popular belief to haunt the waters round the Cape of Good Hope.

Sometime in the late 1500s a Dutch vessel bound for the Pacific was lost without trace. Eventually her wraith was sighted by two Dutch merchantmen rounding the Cape of Good Hope, heading west. Although the weather was good and the sea calm, the ship—henceforth known as the *Flying Dutchman* even though that was not the name on her stern—appeared to be battling her way through a violent gale. From this ghostly sighting the *Flying Dutchman* legend was apparently evolved.[1]

In his *Scènes de la Vie Maritime* (1832), the French author Auguste Jal gives one version of how a Dutch captain (usually the captain of the *Flying Dutchman* is called Vanderdecken) was making a voyage around the Cape of Good Hope when he ran into a head wind 'strong enough to blow the horns off a bull'. Although the ship was in danger, and the passengers pleaded with the captain to turn back or try to seek a port, he laughed at their fears and met their remonstrances with songs of a 'horrible and blasphemous nature'. The ship was buffetted by the wind and the huge waves, and the shattered masts were carried away. Meanwhile the captain sat in his cabin drinking beer and puffing

---

[1]Some scholars aver that the legend arose from the adventures of Bartholomeu Diaz (c 1450-1500), the famous Portuguese navigator. Diaz, of course, is chiefly remembered for his discovery of the Cape of Good Hope in 1487. In his *Os Lusíadas* (1572), Luis Vaz de Camões (c 1524-80) gave the Diaz adventures a somewhat supernatural slant.

at his pipe, openly daring the Almighty to sink him. When the crew and passengers attempted to force the captain to turn, he killed their ringleader and threw him overboard.

'But even as he did so,' writes Jal, 'the clouds opened and a Form alighted on the quarter deck of the ship. This Form is said to have been the Almighty Himself. The crew and passengers were stricken with fear, but the captain went on smoking his pipe, and did not even touch his cap when the Form addressed him.

' "Captain," said the Form, "you are very stubborn."

' "And you are a rascal!" cried the captain. "Who wants a peaceful passage? I don't. I'm asking nothing from you, so clear out of this unless you want your brains blown out."

'So saying, the captain drew a pistol and fired at the Form, but the weapon exploded in his hand. Then the Form told him that henceforth he was accursed, condemned to sail on forever without rest or anchorage or a port of any kind. "Gall," promised the Form, "shall be your drink, and red hot iron your meat. Of your crew, only your cabin boy shall remain with you; horns shall grow out of his forehead, and he shall have the muzzle of a tiger and a skin rougher than that of a dog-fish. And since it is your delight to torment sailors, you shall torment them. For you shall be the evil spirit of the sea, and your ship shall bring misfortune to all who sight it." '

The German legend makes 'Herr von Falkenberg' the hero, and alleges that he is condemned to sail for ever round the North Sea, in a ship without helm or steersman, playing at dice for his soul with the Devil.

Richard Wagner (1813-83), the German composer, used the legend in his opera *Der fliegende Holländer* (1843), but gave his hero absolution from his doom on finding a woman faithful to him till death. Inspiration for the Wagnerian version undoubtedly came from the fictitious *Memoiren des Herrn von Schnabelewopski* (1834) by the German lyric poet Heinrich Heine (1797-1856), to whom in turn it had apparently been suggested by the anonymous tale *Vander-decken's Message Home* in *Blackwood's Edinburgh Magazine* of May 1821. Others say that Heine may have been inspired by Edward Fitzball's melodrama *The Flying Dutchman* (1828), but neither of these English versions allows for the hero's redemption.

Adaptations of the story were also written by Captain Frederick Marryat (1792-1848) in *The Phantom Ship* (1839) and William Clark Russell (1844-1911) in *The Death Ship* (1888). In the version of the *Flying Dutchman* story by Sir Walter Scott (1771-1832) the phantom ship is loaded with gold. A murder is committed on board and a plague breaks out, all adding to the captain's eternal damnation.

Thus the basic story spread and the *Flying Dutchman's* evil ways became legion; he was deemed to have been responsible for casting many a ship into uncharted waters, or to have led them on to rocks and then mocked them. He might turn wine into vinegar, runs another superstition, or curdle all the ship's food into rotting beans. Sometimes he would draw innocently alongside a ship and send letters aboard. If the letters were read, of course, the ship was lost.

Occasionally, the superstitious sailors said, an empty phantom boat would be seen to cast off from the *Flying Dutchman* and draw alongside—a sure sign of misfortune. Perhaps worst of all, Captain Vanderdecken would change the appearance of his ship so that it could not be recognised until it was too late.

Some sailors' tales held that the evil captain had repented, and that he could be seen standing bareheaded on his quarter deck, crying to God for mercy, while his crew of skeletons grinned in the rigging and crammed on more sail.

The *Flying Dutchman* has been variously claimed to be a four-master, a schooner and a brig. Some sea historians even make her the wraith of the Dutch East Indiaman, the *Libera Nos*, commanded by Captain Bernard Fokke, who was well known in the seventeenth century as a skilled and rather daring mariner. In order to make port in record time, Fokke was said to have played dice with the Devil. He is reported to have obtained from the Devil the idea of strengthening the masts of his ship with iron, so that a maximum amount of sail could be carried. Crewed by skeletons, the wraith of the *Libera Nos* is alleged to have been sighted on a number of occasions down the ages. Usually her master is seen as a skeleton standing on the fo'c'sle counting off the centuries with an hourglass.

Among the ghost stories connected with the *Flying Dutchman*, the following are perhaps the most persistent and interesting.

On May 4 1866 the sailing ship *General Grant*, out of Melbourne, Australia, bound for London and under the command of Captain Loughlin,[2] was making good headway. For no apparent reason, however, on May 13 she found herself becalmed in the wide region between the tropics of Cancer and Capricorn known for its good trade winds. Somehow she drove on, as if impelled by some unseen force, until she piled up in a huge cavern under the tall headlands of Disappointment Island.[3] For several nights previous to her wrecking the *General Grant* had been followed by a mystery ship; many on board believed that their pursuer was the *Flying Dutchman*.

In the cabin safe, Captain Loughlin had been carrying some $1,000,000 worth of gold dust on consignment to London agents, and thus the *General Grant* became an attractive prize for salvagers. Various salvage expeditions were organised but none was successful.

During March 1870, the 48-ton schooner *Daphne*, under the command of Captain Jim Wallace and with David

---

[2]See: Armstrong, Warren. *Last Voyage* (Muller, London 1958).

[3]For 300 years, sailors visiting this oblong area between Okinawa, in the Ryukyu Archipelago, Disappointment Island, just south of the Marquesas, Hawaii and the Solomon Islands have reported many ghostly sightings; more per square mile of sea than in any other place on earth.

Ashworth, one of the few survivors from the *General Grant* on board, sailed out of Invercargill (South Island, New Zealand) bound for Disappointment Island. On anchoring near their objective, Wallace, Ashworth and three seamen put out from the *Daphne* to locate the exact position of the submerged *General Grant* and the gold. They were seen to locate the cavern and enter it—but they never returned!

When the *Daphne* finally made home port, the crew testified that, as they lay at anchor, a ghost ship (ie, the *Flying Dutchman*) appeared and bore down on them. Almost colliding, the phantom crossed the schooner's bows and then dissolved into a grey haze. No one believed their story, but in 1958 another firm from London made to salvage the *General Grant*. They too lived through a similar experience.

On her cruise with Admiral Lord Clanwilliam's Detached Squadron (September 14 1880—August 5 1882), the British armoured corvette *Bacchante* also encountered the *Flying Dutchman*. This is the account from a formal entry in the ship's log:

'*July* 11 1881. During the middle watch the so-called *Flying Dutchman* crossed our bows. She first appeared as a strange red light, as of a ship all aglow, in the midst of which light her masts, spars and sails, seemingly those of a normal brig, some two hundred yards distant from us, stood out in strong relief as she came up. Our lookout man on the forecastle reported her as close to our port bow, where also the officer of the watch from the bridge clearly saw her, as did our quarterdeck midshipman, who was sent forward at once to the forecastle to report back. But on reaching there, no vestige nor any sign of any material ship was to be seen either near or away to the horizon. The early morning, as the night had been, was clear, the sea strangely calm. Thirteen persons altogether saw her but whether it was the *Flying Dutchman* or one of the other few alleged phantom ships which are reputed to haunt this area must remain unknown. *Tourmaline* and *Cleopatra*, which were sailing on our starboard quarter, flashed signals asking whether we had seen the strange glow, and if we could account for it.

'During the forenoon watch the seaman who had this morning first reported this phantom vessel fell from our fore-topmast crosstrees and was killed instantly. Towards the end of the afternoon watch, after quarters, our ship was hove-to with headyards aback while we buried him. He was a smart royalyard seaman, one of the most promising hands in the ship, and every man on board feels sad and despondent at his loss.'

To give the incident a more macabre conclusion, when the squadron reached port the commander was mysteriously stricken with a fatal illness. At the time of the encounter, serving aboard the *Inconstant*[4] as midshipmen were Prince George (later King George V 1865-1936) and his brother Prince Albert Victor, Duke of Clarence (1864-92)[5].

The newspapers of the time recorded sightings of the *Flying Dutchman* in 1893, 1905 and 1911, but one of the most authentic stories was given in the late 1890s. Again it concerned a lost treasure ship.

Homeward bound with a mixed freight of consumer goods and some million dollars in gold bullion, the steamship *Hannah Regan* lost a propeller off Okinawa and was further badly damaged by ensuing heavy weather. While efforts were made for the ship to limp home, the propeller shaft broke off and the *Hannah Regan* sank. Some weeks later the bodies of the captain, the first mate and four of the crew were found drifting in an open boat. The captain's journal is the only record of the tragedy.

Later the wreck of the *Hannah Regan* was located on the seabed by a San Francisco tug and a salvage operation began.

---

[4]The two princes were originally serving aboard the *Bacchante* but were transferred to the *Inconstant* when the former developed rudder trouble.

[5]See: Nicolson, Harold. *King George V: His Life and Reign*. (Constable, London 1952). 19-31.

From the official report of this salvage operation the following narrative of the captain is of interest:

'It was a fine, calm and clear night, and after the days of hard exertion by all hands I had ordered them (the salvage workers) to rest before the arduous work that would be expected of us the following day. I myself was about to retire to my own cabin and snatch a few hours sleep but I felt the need of a quiet walk around the deck. I had taken a couple of turns, and could see in the bright moonlight our marker buoys locating the wreck, and was thinking of the tragedy that had overwhelmed her and all aboard when my attention was drawn to what I at first thought was a peculiar shadow some half-mile distant from my ship. I watched it closely for some time and then, to my astonishment, the shadow assumed the shape and appearance of a sailing vessel, clearly distinguishable but of a type which had not sailed the seas for at least two hundred years. There could be no mistaking it. She was headed in our direction, and driving along as if in the grip of violent winds, yet she carried no sail. I stood spellbound. She rolled heavily at times though the seas were flat and calm; and she looked to be sinking by the stern. I was about to shout, to summon help, for it looked as if she could not help running us down, but then it flashed in my mind that this were a phantom and no material vessel.'

The captain held his ground and continued to watch.

'The spectral ship came on, her starboard quarter almost awash and with masses of heavy water pouring over her. She came right alongside, and then I doubted my own shocked senses, for I could see right through her, though every detail of her deck work and her rigging stood out clearly. Two of her boats were hanging from their falls and dragged alongside; so she passed us by, still lower at the stern, and in such a way *disappeared beneath the sea.*'

Next morning the salvage crew continued their work. And then the misfortunes associated with a sighting of the

Flying Dutchman began to take place. The skipper, in his own log, takes up the story:

'This was no simple job, though the wreck was lying in less than ten fathoms, the seas crystal clear so that I was able to watch my divers. I saw one man like a cat climbing the sloping roof haul himself carefully along the broken hull, hand over hand. He made it. With him he carried a charge of gun-cotton to breach the jammed door of the captain's cabin and so get at the safe containing the bullion. He disappeared from my sight and seconds seemed to drag past like minutes, the minutes into hours, and still no sign of the diver, still no explosion I waited for. A second diver went down to investigate, and some time later surfaced to report that the first man's airpipe had become entangled in wreckage and had been cut. The second diver returned to help his comrade, and we waited for two heartbreaking hours before we were ready to acknowledge their death.'

To the superstitious aboard, the *Hannah Regan* was tainted with evil brought on by the *Flying Dutchman's* influence. The tug returned to San Francisco leaving the *Hannah Regan* to rot on the seabed and her gold to sink in the sand.

In more recent times the *Flying Dutchman* has been sighted again. Adolf Hitler's former commander-in-chief of U-boats, Admiral Karl Doenitz, made this entry in a report:

'Certain of my U-boat crews claimed they saw the *Flying Dutchman* or some other so-called phantom ship on their tours of duty east of Suez. When they returned to their base the men said they preferred facing the combined strength of Allied warships in the North Atlantic than know the terror a second time of being confronted by a phantom vessel.[6]'

---

[6]See: Lötzke, H and Brather, H-S. *Übersicht über die Bestände des Deutschen Zentralarchivs Potsdam* (Berlin 1957). Deutsches Zentralarchiv, Potsdam.

Chapter 2

The Kaiser's Haunted Submarine

On May 7 1915, Kapitänleutnant Walther Schwieger, commanding the German submarine (*Unterseebooten*) U-20, sank the 32,500-ton liner *Lusitania* off the coast of Ireland with the loss of 1,198 passengers and crew[1]. Only then, as the world's newspapers spread the horror of the sinking, did the man in the street begin to understand the submarine's war potential.

When Great Britain entered World War I, she had no effective anti-submarine weapon; ramming, or spraying machine-gun bullets at periscopes, was the best that the Royal Navy could do. Thus, even though the British Grand Fleet was superior to Germany's High Seas Fleet (she had 20 modern battleships and four cruisers to Germany's 13 battleships and three battle cruisers) Germany realised her early advantage.

Encouraged by such as Admiral Reinhard Scheer[2], Kaiser William II (1859-1941) therefore charged Admiral Eduard von Capelle[3] with the responsibility of building and

---

[1]Although Germany had warned the *Lusitania* against sailing, her captain failed to take any precautions and did not zigzag in the prescribed manner. Hence the ship fell an easy prey to the German submarine.

[2]The enterprising Commander of the German High Seas Fleet, who had felt it his duty to admit to the Kaiser that 'there can be no doubt that even the most successful result of a high seas battle will not compel England to make peace . . . A victorious end to the war at a not too distant date can only be looked for by the crushing of English economic life through U-boat action . . .'

[3]Von Capelle (1855-1931) was the former Chief of the Navy Office who succeeded Grand Admiral Alfred von Tirpitz (1849-1930) as Secretary of the Imperial German Navy. Von Capelle served in this capacity from March 1916 to September 1918.

increasing the U-boat fleet. Von Capelle delegated some of the responsibility for fast, increased submarine construction in the captured shipyards of Bruges, Belgium, to a subordinate, Admiral Schroeder. From the German naval archives[4] on the construction of this Flanders flotilla comes one of the most curious sea phantom stories of modern times.

During one tour of inspection in the early autumn of 1916, Admiral Schroeder was informed of the teething troubles of U-65, which was one of 24 new craft he was shortly to launch. Apparently U-65 had been a 'magnet for accidents' since early on in her construction. Soon after her keel was laid a heavy girder had slipped from its slings, crashing on the slipway to kill a workman; another died of injuries on his way to hospital. Weeks later when the U-boat was nearly completed, her engine-room became choked with fumes and three more men died.

For reasons of morale, German Naval Security made sure that these incidents were not publicly reported. Satisfied that U-65 had not caused morale-damaging superstitious gossip among the flotilla crews, Admiral Schroeder officially launched the submarines, which immediately made for trials in the North Sea.

By mid-afternoon on the day of launching the new flotilla reached its exercise area off the small island of Noordbeveland, at the entrance of the Ooster Schelde. Here the weather worsened, promising a rough passage.

Aboard the U-65 the commander made preparations for the ship's first dive. A complete inspection of the submarine was made and the commander ordered one of his more experienced crew members to inspect the forward part of the hull. The man clambered out of the conning tower and, to the astonishment and horror of the officers watching, deliberately walked overboard! Fearing that this might unnerve the rest of the crew, the commander decided to act

---

[4]See: Institute für Zeitgeschiche, München.

quickly. He ordered another thorough check of the U-boat's valves and compartments. When the last hatch clips were secured he gave the command, 'Dive! Dive! Dive!'

All went well and the U-boat settled easily on the seabed. The commander completed his exercise log and then gave the order to surface. But the U-65 would not respond to the controls! For the next 12 hours or so she lay immovable on the seabed; eventually water entered her hull and reached the batteries, the air became poisoned with deadly fumes. At the point when the crew were more dead than alive, the U-boat surfaced.

U-65 returned with the rest of the flotilla to Bruges to take on supplies and torpedoes for her first operational tour of duty. Sometime after the torpedoes had been loaded, one exploded, killing the ship's second lieutenant and five enlisted men. A report was sent to Admiral Schroeder who ordered extensive repairs in dry dock. To date the U-65 had been the cause of the death of 12 men—but worse was to come!

While the U-65's first lieutenant was in the wardroom on evening, the door burst open and a fear-crazed petty officer collapsed on the floor. Once revived, the petty officer stammered that he had seen the ghost of the second lieutenant, who had been instantly killed in the torpedo blast, come aboard. The petty officer's story was confirmed by another seaman: 'Yes, Herr Oberleutnant. We saw him come aboard and walk slowly to the bows; and there he stood, arms folded across his chest, staring at us.'

Both men subsequently appeared before the U-65's commander, who swore them to secrecy: 'You will say nothing whatever in any place or to anybody, of this regrettable incident, you understand? If you disobey this order I shall place you under arrest. It is my belief that somebody has perpetrated a practical joke. Either that or it could be the work of British secret agents seeking to harm the morale of our submarine crews. If that is the game, we shall see!'

Two days later Pedersen, one of the men who had seen the second lieutenant's ghost, deserted.

Soon afterwards U-65 left her Bruges base and, negotiating the Dover Straits barrage, made her first enemy 'kill' off the Kent coast. The following day she surfaced off the British naval base of Portland, Dorset, and while lookouts on port stations and conning tower scanned the sea, her batteries were charged.

An hour or so passed without any unusual occurrence. Then, shaking with fright, his face pale with terror, the starboard lookout screamed to the first lieutenant: 'Look, look, the ghost . . . its arms are folded like Pedersen described, silent, not moving, though the seas sweep across the ship. It's not one of us. It's the dead second officer!'

Noticeably shaken himself, the first lieutenant shouted to the mysterious figure on the bows. The figure turned round and stared at the officer, who could see in the fading light the features of his dead colleague, now lying buried in the naval cemetery at Wilhelmshaven. The first lieutenant summoned the commander and both men watched until the phantom had disappeared. Even though the next few days were packed with action for the crew (the U-65 overtook and torpedoed a large supply ship heading for Plymouth, and crippled a second with gunfire), they were clearly frightened by the phantom and frequently paused to look over their shoulders in apprehensive anticipation.

On returning to base U-65 found the Bruges naval yards under heavy Allied fire. Quickly disembarking the crew ran for shelter. As he sprinted across the dockyard the commander of U-65 was killed by shrapnel. Moments later an enlisted man stumbled down the steps of the air-raid shelter crying that he had seen the dead second lieutenant's phantom again on the U-boat's bows!

Annoyed by the reports of ghostly disturbances on board U-65, Admiral Schroeder ordered a complete enquiry into the phantom sightings. Each member of the crew was questioned and Schroeder made a personal inspection of the submarine. Nothing unusual was found, but as an extra precaution the admiral had a Lutheran chaplain conduct a service to exorcise any evil spirits which might still be lingering aboard the jinxed U-boat.

Under a new commander, U-65 did sterling work for the German war effort in destroying much tonnage of the Allied merchant ships. For some considerable time there were no reports of ghostly sightings. Eventually command of U-65 was given to Oberleutnant Schelle who replaced the 'hard-bitten, no-nonsense' commander who had deployed the submarine so well against the Allies. Even though this latter commander had forbidden the mention of ghosts aboard his submarine, a chief petty officer made this comment in a letter home:

'We were never a pack of nervous fools, and we have known from the first day we served in the ship that there was something evil about her. Not one of us ever put name to it, nor understood these frightening experiences, but we never thought we saw the ghost; we never imagined anything. What we saw, we saw, and that is all. I am among many members of our present crew who have seen the wraith of our dead second officer, standing always in the bows, with his arms folded. One night, lying sleepless in my bunk, I watched terrified as the phantom entered my quarters and then walked past me and disappeared into our forward torpedo room. It never came out again. He never knew it, but on many occasions I saw our previous commander, the man who threatened us with punishment if we so much as mentioned the word 'ghost', look over his shoulder and tremble. It was not until he handed over command to Schelle that I heard from his steward that he declared the ship to be haunted. I am due to sail in the U-65 for her next tour of duty, but I pray that I may be stricken by some severe illness, or wounded in action and taken into a hospital, so that I may live to tell my story one day.'

During the May of 1918, U-65 was sent to the Bay of Biscay to harry, intercept and destroy an important Allied convoy. Off Finistere, Eberhardt, the U-65's leading gunner, went berserk, screaming that he had brushed shoulders with the ghost of the second lieutenant. Eberhardt was sedated and put under guard but, reviving, he managed to outwit his guard, escaped and committed suicide.

That night the engineer lieutenant broke his leg and developed a high fever. Shortly after dawn, as the U-boat surfaced on her way to search for the convoy, Petty Officer Richard Meyer, for no apparent reason, jumped into the sea and swam from sight!

By nightfall the convoy had been sighted, and in the ensuing conflict depth charges sent U-65 hurtling to the seabed. Thereafter the submarine 'seemed to go mad'. An eerie greenish-white light glowed through the vessel and one sailor shouted, '*Herr Gott*! It's here—here at my side! I can feel its cold fingers touching my cheek!'

Miraculously, the commander was able to nurse his crippled submarine back to base. Schroeder was told of the further ghostly happenings aboard U-65. Immediately the commander was relieved and an entirely new crew selected for operations after the submarine had left dry dock following a refitting.

On the morning of July 10 1918, somewhere off Cape Clear, an American submarine was patrolling at periscope depth when a mysterious object was sighted. Closing for investigation the American submarine saw that the object was, in fact, a derelict, unmanned German U-boat—and on the side of the U-boat could be read the lettering 'U-65'. The American submarine closed in further with torpedoes ready for firing but, before they could be fired, an explosion was seen to erupt from the U-65, which sank. Before the U-boat disappeared, however, the American commander had witnessed a strange sight through his periscope: on the bows of the U-boat the figure of a man appeared with arms folded standing motionless. As the U-boat disappeared below the waves the man vanished into thin air!

On July 31 1918, German Naval Headquarters issued this communiqué:

'One of our submarines, the U-65, is missing and must be presumed lost with thirty-four officers and men.'

Nothing more was publicly reported about the ill-fated U-65, but the well-known German psychologist, Professor Hecht, investigated the case. In an official survey published of his findings (details of which were never publicised) Hecht said, 'This phenomena does not lend itself to any explanation. I can put forward no alternative theory to the supernatural agency which finally brought about the destruction of this ill-fated vessel'[5].

More than half a century later the verdict is still open!

---

[5]See records in: Staatsbibliothek der Stiftung Preussischer Kulturbesitz, Marburg, GFR.

Chapter 3

The Case
of the Phantom Killer

The 11,346-ton cruise ship *Llanstephan Castle* was built in 1914 at Govan, Scotland, for Great Britain's famous Union-Castle Line. Designed to carry 229 first-class and 202 tourist class passengers, the liner served as a troop ship during World War I. During the period 1919-39, the liner was on the London-East Africa run, and it was during one of these trips that her jinx turned into a phantom killer.

During the summer of 1938 on a voyage round Africa, a level-headed lady artist from Northern Ireland was aboard the *Llanstephan Castle*. In a letter to a friend she left this personal testimony of the phantom:

'For some months I had wanted to make a long cruise and see something of places I had never visited before, so I booked a cabin in the *Llanstephan Castle*, intending to exchange the wet, cold and long winter of Ireland for some weeks of sunshine. The advent of the Munich crisis (Adolf Hitler's threat to Czechoslovakia) for a while made it problematical whether the cruise would in fact take place, but as events proved, the international crisis was settled temporarily and I reached London to do some shopping before going abroad.

'We embarked at Tilbury on a damp and dismal day. About three days later we encountered bad weather and the ship was badly battered by heavy seas, a considerable amount of damage being done to her fittings, and three members of the crew were injured. An officer told me he had never known conditions like this in the many years he had been in the service; and at Gibraltar the weather

The most famous of all phantom ships is the *Flying Dutchman*, whose blaspheming captain was doomed to sail the seas eternally. Versions of its appearances are found in novels and poems. Wagner drew the inspiration for his opera *Der fliegende Holländer* from these old tales. (*Mansell Collection.*)

The haunted German submarine *U-65*. The ship's morale was low because of psychic happenings, and caused Admiral Schroeder many administrative difficulties. (*Author's Collection.*)

The 11,346-ton cruise ship *Llanstephan Castle*. During her trip round Africa in 1938 a 'phantom killer' was reported aboard. (*The Union-Castle Steamship Co Ltd.*)

The German-built, 10,000-ton Merchant Navy Ship *Asiatic Prince* went missing in mysterious circumstances in the Pacific in 1928. (*Author's Collection.*)

The world's biggest sailing-ship, the five-masted *Köbenhavn* was built in 1924. She disappeared on the Australia run. (*Author's Collection.*)

A 'ghost ship' off the south coast of England. The idea of a ship as a living entity resulted in many tales of phantom craft. (*Harry Price Library, University of London.*)

continued so rough that it was impossible for any passengers to go ashore. A Naval hospital tender came alongside us and removed the injured seamen.

'That evening, my steward told me that the liner had for some two years been considered unlucky and that strange things were continually happening aboard, but I dismissed the story as imagination on the part of a rather badly rattled man. But he was quite serious; he said there had been a suicide aboard in the course of the last three voyages, and accidents which ought never to have happened. Then he said: "Maybe I should not mention these things. I'm sorry."

'I dismissed it from mind, for there was quite a lot to prepare for, the ship being scheduled to call at Tangier and then Genoa. I dined at the chief officer's table together with six other passengers but we never seemed able to really get together; nor for that matter did any other passengers, and it was as if an air of oppression surrounded us all. I could not define it, but it was apparent. We sailed from Genoa for Port Said, where I went ashore with one or two other folk and made the usual round of sight-seeing tours.

'We sailed through the Suez Canal and finally reached Beira; but still that strange, heavy atmosphere prevailed. It wasn't the heat, which was oppressive, but something that seemed to wrap itself around the ship and all aboard. On the way south to Durban, in perfectly calm seas, the ship suddenly developed an alarming list and it was suggested that the cargo was shifted. I asked the chief officer whether any danger existed, but he laughed and replied that the chief steward was to blame for broaching and emptying the freshwater storage tanks on one side of the ship without any thought for trimming the vessel. It seemed a strange explanation to me, but I could not dispute it.

'When we reached Durban, however, I was told that a member of the ship's catering department had disappeared and it was thought had deserted the ship. It was after leaving Durban that I went out on deck around eleven o'clock at night, being unable to sleep and thinking that a walk around the upper promenade deck might make me want to go to bed. Nobody else was in sight and all I could see was the dim light burning over the main entrance to the saloon. I stopped walking and looked up at the sky; it was a lovely night. And then something indistinct approached me; it moved slowly and with what seemed to be a cold purpose. And as it came nearer I saw that it was the figure of a man in uniform, and that the clothing was dripping with some strange greenish slime. I knew then, why I cannot say, that it intended taking hold of me and pushing me over the ship's rail, and I was so terrified, I was unable to move or to call for help.

'The thought seemed to come to my mind—what would my family think? For I had no reason to commit suicide. I tried to move. I prayed. There is no shame in admitting that. I prayed as I had never done before.

'Then I found I was able to move, and I ran as fast as I could toward the bow of the ship and finally reached my cabin in a roundabout manner. There was a window, not just a round porthole, over my bed and it was open about six inches. I flung myself at it and tried to close it, but something on deck outside prevented me doing so. How long I stood there I cannot say, but in time I reopened my cabin door and ran across to the nearby bathroom; somehow I thought I would be safer locked in there. And as I locked the door I knew that this thing in tattered uniform was with me. I managed to unlock the door and fled back to my cabin. The window was still open, and I watched the fingers of a hand take hold of the upper sash. I ran from the cabin again and managed to reach the cabin of a woman friend and there I spent the rest of the terrifying night.

'I was far too frightened by the experience to talk about it to anybody, and we reached Tenerife. Two days later the ship's doctor was on deck at around 10.00 pm and discovered

38

a woman passenger poised on the ship's rail, dressed in a negligee, about to leap overboard. He dragged her to safety and kept her in his care until the ship returned to Southampton; but I am certain that the ship's doctor did not see that unspeakable thing which had failed to kill me and was trying to kill this second woman.'[1]

The *Llanstephan Castle* was refitted in Belfast in World War II and went back into the Africa service. She was sold for breaking in March 1952.

---

[1]See: Armstrong, Warren. *Sea Phantoms*. (Odhams, London 1956).

Chapter 4

American Sea Phantoms

The Case of the Headless Sailor

For more than sixty years the late Elliott O'Donnell, Britain's ghost-hunter extraordinary, actively pursued his investigations into phantoms on both sides of the Atlantic. While at the International Hotel, San Francisco, O'Donnell met a Captain Harding, the master of a trader, who gave him the background to a strange affair concerning a Norwegian vessel called the *Squando*; a case which O'Donnell believed to be unique in maritime history.

A few years prior to O'Donnell's encounter, the first mate of the *Squando* had been murdered one night as the ship lay in San Francisco harbour. Later the mate's decapitated body had been found floating in the harbour. It transpired that the captain of the *Squando* and his wife had formed an intense dislike of the first mate. One evening they both had plied the mate with drink. When he was drunk and incapable the woman had held the mate's arms while the husband decapitated him with an axe. Then they heaved the corpse overboard. Captain Harding strongly believed that the mate had been the woman's lover, and that, fearing they might be found out, the woman had pretended to her husband that the mate had been persistently annoying her.

Soon after the murder, it seems, while at sea, the crew mutinied and the new captain, appointed in the murderer's place, was killed. The cause of the mutiny was never made clear, but it is thought probable that some quarrel had broken out with the captain over some odd happenings aboard the *Squando* relating to the ghost of the murdered sailor. Thereafter the *Squando* acquired a sinister reputation, which was only heightened when her next captain was found dead in unaccountable circumstances. His successor also died in a very mysterious fashion.

After the fourth death the hauntings aboard the *Squando* proved to be too much for the crew, who on the vessel's arrival at Bathurst, New Brunswick, in the spring of 1893, deserted to a man. Efforts to obtain another crew proved unsuccessful and the *Squando* lay idle for a long time. Eventually, the rumours about the ship's hauntings reached the Norwegian Consul, who decided to investigate. He hired two burly, hard-headed seamen as night watchmen and gave them instructions to hide aboard the *Squando* and watch for anything strange. Anyone suspected of playing tricks on the ship was to be seized.

The two men rowed out to the *Squando* and began their vigil in the captain's cabin around 9.00 pm. Up to 10.00 pm nothing happened, and just as the two men were beginning to doubt the stories of the hauntings, they suddenly heard strange noises on deck. They ran to the companion ladder and climbed on deck, to find it in great disorder. When they had boarded, everything had been neatly in its place. Now spars, ropes, yards, hand-spikes and barrels littered the deck, but no-one was to be seen. Somewhat puzzled, the two men went below again, and prepared to retire for the night.

They had not been asleep long when they were both awakened by someone tugging at their sleeves; yet, when they sat up, no-one was there. But that was not all! As the men climbed out of their bunks, unseen, cold hands brushed their faces and a hollow whisper rang through the cabin— 'Go, go, at once!'

By this time the men were convinced that they were dealing with the supernatural and made to quit the ship. As they ran along the deck to where their boat was moored they heard a crash behind them. Turning round they saw, in the pale misty light, a headless figure coming towards them. The two men fled in terror. The next night two more men were hired for a vigil—but they too ran off in terror. This was to happen on a number of occasions, until no-one would board the *Squando* after dark. Finally the *Squando* was abandoned and sold, headless ghost and all, to the ship-breakers.

A New Haven Apparition

From New Haven, the busy city port of Connecticut, comes this story of a strange apparition witnessed by a large crowd of men, women and children. In his tract *Magnalia Christi Americana*, the Rev Cotton Mather (1663-1728) recounted the story which had dated from January 1647:

'We had suffered hereabouts in New Haven a series of depressing reverses in trade and industry, so we sought to retrieve ourselves by building a 150-ton ship to freight her for England. Our fine vessel sailed away manned by the best and bravest of our town, but one slow month followed another and we had no tidings of its arrival overseas. We were sadly distraught until, one day, after a great thunder-storm about one hour before sunset, a ship of exactly like dimensions, with her canvas and colours set, appeared in the air coming up the harbour against the wind for the space of one hour. Among us was the Revd Mr Pierpoint who had been called to behold this great work of the Lord; yea, our very children cried out, *"There* is a brave ship!"* When so near that any one of our number might easily hurl a stone on board, the vessel's main top seemed blown off, then her mizzentop, then her masting was blown away; before our wondering eyes she overset and so vanished completely into a smoky cloud. The vision was given, we know, that we might now understand the tragic end of our first deep-sea ship and of our friends in her.'

What the goodfolk of New Haven had undoubtedly seen was a sea-mirage, in which a vessel below the horizon can sometimes be seen plainly in the air above it. Mirage of course, is a word used to describe optical phenomena that arise from the reflection and refraction of light in unusual circumstances. Mirages are *chiefly* seen at sea, or in deserts, where there is calm air that is either extremely hot or extremely cold. Sea-mirage has been responsible for a number of remarkable 'ghost' sightings, many of which are recorded in the histories of the American Merchant Marine.

In his *Journal* under the date Thursday August 9 1492, Christopher Columbus noted seeing a phantom island in the twilight west of the Canaries. Once again this mirage was caused by atmospheric conditions peculiar to the locality. Some five hundred years later, on August 10 1958, the Madrid newspaper *ABC* reproduced a photograph of this same mirage island. The Anthelion Phenomenon, incidentally, may have caused some shore 'spectres'. This phenomenon is observed by a person whose shadow is cast upon a moist surface, such as a cloud, fog or dewy grass; around the shadow are several concentric rings, luminous and coloured, shading into white at the edge. This occurrence is also known as the 'Brocken Spectre'.

Yachtsmen's Sightings

Any reasonable person would think that there is without fail a rational explanation for the strange happenings at sea, but time after time reason evades us. Mr John S. Schultz of Boston, Massachusetts and his family have no doubts about the phantoms they saw while vacationing aboard their yacht *Yorktown Clipper*.

During the summer of 1967, the Schultz family spent their vacation exploring the New England coast from Montauk Point, Long Island to Mystic, Connecticut. Early one morning, as they were returning home on a wild 200-mile sweep around Georges Bank, they saw a submarine surface a little away from their starboard bow.

Although the sea was rough and plenty of spray from the

bows was sheeting in their faces, the Schultz family clearly saw the name *Thresher* on the side of the submarine. John S. Schultz, however, recognised it as an American submarine and saw that it had a huge gash along the waterline. Puzzled that the submarine was still able to float with such a gash, he nevertheless said nothing to his family on deck watching.

After a while, to their complete amazement and no little fear, the submarine rose maybe a foot or two into the air, jack-knifed stem to stern and then disappeared below the choppy sea. Stranger still was the fact that all this time, the crew and master of the *Yorktown Clipper* were watched through a telescope by a figure of a man dressed in USN uniform on the submarine's walkway, and by another on the bows. Neither man had attempted to climb inside the submarine as she became elevated, and they had both maintained their position while the craft jack-knifed, as if they had been ornamental figureheads.

Needless to say, the Schultz family were greatly perturbed at what they had seen, albeit in the early morning light with the sea spray in their faces; all five, two adults and three children, had watched the same strange enactment.

They all agreed it was best not to say anything about their experience right away, for they thought no-one would believe them, but later John S. Schultz carried out some discreet research among the records of the Marine Historical Association. He did, in fact, find out that there had been an American submarine called *Thresher*.

Apparently, the USN submarine *Thresher* had been a very large vessel of 4,300 tons, when submerged. She had been launched on July 9 1960 as the prototype and name ship of the Thresher Class of nuclear-powered attack submarines. Her reactor had supplied steam to a 15,000 shp steam turbine, which had given a range of 60,000 miles before re-fuelling was necessary. Her surface speed had been 20 knots and 35 knots submerged. The diving hydroplanes were not attached to the main hull but projected from the conning tower which had been situated nearer to the bow than was usual, and which had been called her 'sail'.

After about a year in service, *Thresher* had returned to Portsmouth Naval yard for modification and left on April 9 1963 for deep-diving trials. Although her normal complement was 95 men and officers, she had on board this time 129 persons, of which 17 were civilian technicians.

During this trip *Thresher* was accompanied by the submarine rescue vessel *Skylark* (ex-*USN Yustaga*), with whom she was in constant touch by submarine telephone. On April 10 1963 at 9.12 am, *Thresher* had reported that she was approaching her deep-dive test depth. This, of course, was a routine check, and thereafter the craft was pronounced 'still going well'. A minute or two later, however, came the disjointed report 'have position up angle . . . attempting to blow up . . . ballast tanks'. The curious message was followed by the sound of high pressure air blowing water from the ballast tanks. At 9.17 am another message was received by *Skylark*, but was too disjointed to be understood; this message was also distorted by sounds of breakage.

Thresher's position at the time was near to *Yorktown Clipper's* route where the ghostly sighting was made. The position was about 220 miles east of Cape Cod, where the depth is about 1,400 fathoms. The pressure at this depth would amount to some 3,700 lbs per sq in, so that the submarine must have been crushed to destruction. Officially the cause of the *Thresher* disaster remains a mystery.

Did the Schultz family really see *Thresher* some four years after her complete destruction? Whether it was *Thresher* or not, that family will have a healthy respect for sea phantoms for the rest of their lives!

A similar happening overtook the Roake family of New Bedford, Massachusetts. A few years ago they took their yacht *Gay Gaspard* on a vacational trip north to the east coasts of Canada, eventually to explore the Gulf of St Lawrence, between Quebec and Newfoundland.

The weather was bright and sunny as they passed Mt Desert Island, Maine, and Grand Manan Island, New Brunswick, and a following wind helped them all the way. As they approached Chaleur Bay, New Brunswick, however, the wind dropped and they had to use their engines up past Port Daniel, Chandler and Grande Rivière. By the time they reached Gaspé the wind had risen again and they made good headway round the Cape.

As with the Schultz family of Boston, the Roakes made their sighting during the early morning. Around 7.00 am, Mary Roake brought coffee to her husband at the helm and they stood for a while together discussing the day's route, when an explosion attracted their attention towards the cliffs of Gaspé Bay. To their astonishment they saw a flagship under full sail heading towards the rocks. Identifying the ship as an eighteenth century man-of-war, and begged by the children who had now clambered on deck, to move closer, Pete Roake turned the *Gay Gaspard* towards Gaspé cliffs.

Although the yacht made good headway the man-of-war appeared now to be becalmed. What was it doing there? the kids clamoured. Was it a camera team out on location for a historical sea movie? Closer and closer the *Gay Gaspard* moved to the ship. Now the Roakes could see the British flag on the poop deck and a crowd of redcoated soldiers in mitre-hats on deck. Suddenly the ports of the ship were ablaze with light, and drumbeats were heard, as the mysterious crew were drummed to quarters.

Taking his binoculars out of their case, Pete Roake focused on the mystery ship and crew. As he tried to read the name of the ship, set out on the side in gold letters, the vessel seemed to shudder. Simultaneously a scream was heard across the water and the ship then slowly, but completely, disappeared.

Later, when the yacht was nearer to the shore, the Roakes searched the sea where the ship had been seen; they found nothing, not even floating seaweed. By this time, of course, they realised they had witnessed a sea phantom. For a long time the event puzzled the family until one day, quite by chance, Mary Roake borrowed Le Moine's book *The Legends of the St Lawrence* from a Massachusetts library. On page 36 of this book she found mentioned that a British flagship, sent by Queen Anne (1665-1714) to reduce the French forts, had sunk under the cliffs of Cap d'Espoir in Gaspé Bay— the exact spot where they had seen their phantom ship!

The Missing River Boat

In June 1872, a Mississippi river boat, *The Iron Mountain*, set out on the most mysterious voyage she was ever to make. One of the largest of her kind, with a length in excess of 180 feet, a beam of 35 feet and powered by five boilers, the river boat regularly towed a string of barges from New Orleans to Pittsburg. This particular day she pulled away from her stopping place at Vicksburg, rounded the bend of the river and that was the last anyone ever saw of her. All the crew, passengers and cargo disappeared—all that was left was the string of barges she had been pulling.

Investigation showed that the towrope had been cut, but there was no sign of debris to show that she had floundered and none of the other river boats had seen her (they constantly passed and repassed each other on the river). The strangest thing of all is that none of the 54 persons aboard ever turned up anywhere!

Just north of St Joseph on the Mississippi, however, during the past 90 years fishermen and rivercomers have frequently heard the ghostly cries of a woman coming from the middle of the river. First a scream is heard and then— *Gaston! Gaston! Aidez-moi au nom de Dieu. Les hommes me blessent!* (Gaston! Help me in the name of God. The men are hurting me!) Many around St Joseph, Natchez and Vicksburg believe that the ghostly voice is that of a passenger who was aboard the ill-fated *Iron Mountain* when she met her fate. The fact that the voice mentions men, suggests to some that the boat was mysteriously hijacked, the passengers killed and buried, and the boat dismantled piece by piece. Probably the truth about *The Iron Mountain* will never be known, but those who care listen carefully in case the phantom French-speaking lady's voice tells more.

A Phantom Patrol

The Caribbean islands are full of people who can tell strange stories of phantom ships, but this particular apparition was seen by an American patrol boat, just off the coast of Jamaica. The cruise patrol boat was waiting in a bay not far from the shore to rendezvous with another patrol boat. The night was pitch-black except for the stars, and not a breath of breeze was blowing. About midnight there appeared at the other side of Montego Bay a small schooner, with sails *billowing*, making for the open sea. As there had been rather more smuggling than usual at that time, the patrol cruiser gave chase.

As the cruiser sliced the waves with its powerful motors, the piercing searchlight was swung into position. On the deck of the schooner could be seen several shadowy figures attending to the sails. In a moment the American patrol cruiser was up to the side of the schooner, the officer in charge challenged the schooner captain and the searchlight was played on to her bridge. Seconds later the schooner completely vanished leaving nothing but waves and bits of seaweed. Although he recorded the sighting in his log the cruiser captain could offer no explanation. And still the question is asked in the cocktail bars of Kingston: 'What in fact *had* they seen?'

The Master of The Wilmington Star

The coffee lounge of the Akasaka Tokyu Hotel in Tokyo is a strange location to come across an American sea phantom. Some little time ago, however, I was staying at this hotel close to Tokyo's Akasaka-Mitsuke expressway junction and among the fellow guests was an American gentleman called Thomas Challoner Ridgeway Jr, who hailed from Inglewood, Los Angeles. From Tokyo's English language newspapers he found out that I was interested in the supernatural and, seeking me out, told me the following story, which, he said, was his one and only experience with the unknown. He had not really felt able to relate the story to anyone at length before, but as I was an experienced psychic researcher he felt at ease to tell me. All the facts of his story, he said, could be verified.

Ridgeway explained that New York's Harlem River was not navigable at all, even by small craft, until 1895, when a channel was cut through the shoal called Spuyten Duyvil, at the Hudson end. Apparently the old river course was filled in, and, administratively, a small slice of Manhattan remains within its loop, separated by a vanished geographical fact from its hinterland in the Bronx. Here it was that Thomas C. Ridgeway Jr's maternal grandfather had his scrap-yard.

As a child, Ridgeway had played and scoured amongst such obscure inlets as Saw Mill Creek and Dead Horse Bay, or the shining flats and shallows of Jamaica Bay. But Ridgeway said he saw his sea phantom at his grandfather's yard on the Harlem River.

One day in 1905, he went in search of his young friend Abe Stark, whose father was a longshoreman of well established waterfront pedigree, for this day he had exciting news. Ridgeway's grandfather had bought an old ship for scrap and she was lying in the small dockyard. The scrap men had not yet started to dismantle her, and there was plenty of time to explore the ship before the men arrived. Once Abe was found, the two boys raced in high glee to the busy dock.

From the quaymaster they heard that the ship, *The*

Wilmington Star, classed as a small brig, had not been to sea since 1879. She had been built at a shipyard in the Southern States and had been employed for the greater part of her career in carrying freight between Charleston, South Carolina, Newport News, Virginia and New York. Once a fast craft, as she lay in dock now, the boys agreed that they had never seen a more miserable or dilapidated looking hulk.

Once the boys had clambered aboard *The Wilmington Star*, they found there was little to see. A couple of bare masts protruded from the deck and the door of the deckhouse creaked noisily in the breeze. They descended the companion ladder of the main hatchway, to find the cabins and forecastle just as depressing. Everywhere was swimming with water and the whole place had an eerie silence, only occasionally broken by the splash and scamper of rats.

Somewhat disappointed by their exploration, the boys retraced their steps along the passage leading to the companion ladder, when Abe Stark suddenly tugged at Tom Ridgeway's sleeve: 'Who's that?' he asked, pointing forward. In the half light below, the boys watched a tall man, clad in seaman's costume of a past era, slowly come down the ladder. The sunlight from the deck above slanted on the man's face throwing it into strong relief. He appeared to be a man of around 50 years of age, with very pronounced features, red curly hair, beard and whiskers, but absolutely colourless skin.

The man descended slowly and advanced straight towards the two boys. As he drew near they instinctively shrank against the wall. Not seeming to notice the lads, the man walked past them and entered one of the empty cabins. Rather pale and scared, the boys clambered on deck again and sat on a broken pulley, to regain their breath. Only as their senses began to register again did the boys realise that as the man had passed them he had made no noise! Even though the passageway had been covered by about an inch of water!

Eventually the boys sought out Ridgeway's grandfather and informed him of the man they had seen. But the scrapyard owner only smiled, he knew that the old ship he had bought was haunted and he told the lads the story. Apparently the ghost story had originally commenced on July 21 1861 when the Confederate Army's success at Bull Run ended the Federal hope of an easy victory. Anxious to retain his profits, the then owner of *The Wilmington Star* regularly changed the flag at his mainmast to suit the waters he was in; while in the South he flew the Confederate flag, and in the North the Union flag. As an extra precaution the owner had forged a separate log book to suit each shipping authority and in the captain's cabin a set of false nameplates were kept (showing the name *New York Dandy*) for Union waters.

One hot sultry night then, in mid-July 1861, *The Wilmington Star* lay at anchor for the night off Chincoteague Bay, Maryland. For some reason or other the captain, Josiah Marchmont, and the first mate, Andrew Garratty, had gone ashore, and the crew were at their ease. Not long after the second dog watch the lookout was startled by a prolonged scream which seemed to come from the shore. The lookout aroused his mates and described what he had heard.

Later, as a group of them looked seawards their attention was attracted by a noise on the bridge. Turning, they saw Captain Marchmont slowly descending the bridge steps. In the moonlight they clearly saw his red beard and whiskers. On this occasion, however, the captain looked very pale and made no reply to their salutes of 'Good evening, sir.' Instead he pushed past them, went straight to his cabin and slammed the door.

Just then the second mate descended the companionway and the men joked, 'Watch out, the captain's back'.

The mate stared at them, 'What do you mean?' he asked.

'The captain's back,' the men repeated. 'When did he come aboard?'

The mate's face hardened. 'He hasn't come aboard. Here,

are you trying to have me on?' he growled.

The seamen explained that they had just seen the captain go into his cabin. But the second mate insisted that the captain and the first mate had not yet returned. To satisfy himself, however, he knocked on the captain's door. There was no reply. The officer slowly opened the door to find the cabin empty.

Next morning there was still no sign of the two officers and the ship was obliged to sail for New York without them. Later the company owning *The Wilmington Star* appointed a new captain and first mate.

Captain Marchmont and his first mate were never seen again in the flesh, but the captain's wraith was a continual visitor to *The Wilmington Star* whenever she was near that strip of coast between Ocean City, Maryland and Cape Charles, Virginia. No-one ever found out what really happened to the two men, but several had their suspicions. According to gossip, an expatriot Irish bawd owned and operated a bordello in the area of Chincoteague Bay around the 1860s. She had a reputation for luring sailors into the bordello, robbing them and throwing their bodies into a well. Many believed that this had been the fate of Captain Marchmont and the first mate Garratty.

Some Phantom Ships of Florida

At the end of the Seminole Indian Wars in 1858, there were roughly 150 Indians left in Florida. Now the Seminoles (meaning 'separatists', 'runaways') descendants of the Creek Confederacy, have increased tenfold and have retained their identity and customs. As late as the 1950s the ways of the Seminoles had changed little. In their two languages, Miccosukee of the area to the south of Lake Okeechobee, and Creek to the north, they retold tales of the Sea Spirits which once ruled the coast of Florida from Fernandina Beach, round Biscayne Bay, Florida Bay and Little Sable

One of Britain's 'Class A' submarines, *HMS Affray,* was wrecked in 1951. The cause of her disappearance was a complete mystery. (*Wright & Logan, Naval Photographers.*)

The United States submarine *Thresher* was 4,300 tons when submerged. Her ghost was reputedly seen at the spot where she sank. (*Dept of Defense, Washington, USA.*)

The 32,500-ton liner, *Lusitania*, at full speed. She was sunk by a German U-boat in 1915, with great loss of life. (*National Maritime Museum*.)

The Goodwin Sands, the most notorious of Britain's ship hazards. The 2,327 ton Italian vessel *Silvia Onorato* struck the Goodwins in January 1948. (*The Daily Sketch*.)

Portrait of Horatio Herbert Earl Kitchener of Khartoum and of Broome (1850-1916), by H. von Herkomer and F. Goodall (1890). He died when the cruiser *Hampshire* ran into bad weather off the Orkneys and sank with all hands. (*National Portrait Gallery, London.*)

The drum which Sir Francis Drake took with him on his voyage round the world. It is said to sound when England is in danger, to summon his protective wraith. It was probably beaten in 1596 when he was buried at sea. (*By courtesy of the City Museums, Plymouth.*)

The lighthouse of Eilean Mor in the Flannan Islands, also called the Seven Hunters. The scene of an intriguing lighthouse mystery in which three men disappeared, the story still defies solution. (*Author's Collection.*)

Gateway to the ruined Cistercian abbey at Beaulieu, Hampshire, which was founded by King John in 1204. The Early English refectory is now the parish church. Said to be haunted by monks who make their way towards it from the neighbouring coast. (*The British Tourist Authority.*)

Creek to the Ten Thousand Islands near Cape Romano and up to Apalachicola and Pensacola. Among those spectres which haunted the swamplands and everglades was the Seminole adaptation of the Trickster Spirit which was to be later immortalised in Joel Chandler Harris' (1848-1908) stories of Brer Rabbit (see: *A Book of Witchcraft*).

Strangely enough the sea phantoms most often quoted by the modern Seminoles are not of their own mythology, but relics of the white man. One story in particular concerns the phantom bark of a bearded Spanish pirate, which is persistently seen in the region of Whitewater Bay in the heart of the Everglades National Park. One ghostly sea phantom popular with tourists, lies a little further to the south, however, alongside 'sunshine alley', the world's longest ocean-going highway which links Florida mainland with Key West.

On the Conch and Molasses Reefs of the Florida Keys (those amazing limestone-and-coral stepping-stones that march south-westward from Barnes Sound, separating the Straits of Florida from Florida Bay and the Gulf of Mexico) lie the wrecks of the *San Joseph y las Animas* and the *Benwood*. Of these two wrecks the former has become famous for its ghosts.

Following the migrating Indians to the Florida Keys, the Spaniards came to loot the New World which Christopher Columbus had found them. Soon, however, the Florida Keys became a storm-wracked gauntlet between the riches of plundered Mexico and Peru, and the king's coffers in Madrid. One day above all others was to be remembered in Spanish naval history.

On Friday June 13 1733, a Spanish fleet of merchant ships set out from Cuba bound for Spain. Aboard was the two-year output of Mexico City's mint: a fabulous treasure. The rapacious Spaniards had hardly left Havana Harbour when a gale struck their fleet. By June 15 1733 the ships were off Plantation Key, and struggling for their lives against the full force of a southeasterly hurricane. The *Boston Weekly News Letter* of September 1733 broadcast their fate: '. . . lately the Spanish Flota consisting of 21 Sail of Ships (4 whereof were Men of War) were all cast on shoar upon the Coast of Florida . . . the Spaniards have saved 12 Million pieces of Eight, and carried the same to the Havanna with other Merchandises, Rigging &c . . .'

Among the ill-fated Spanish fleet was the 190-foot Spanish merchantman, *San Joseph y las Animas*. From time to time, over the next 200 years, fishermen and yachtsmen from Upper Matecumbe Key, Islamorada, Windley Key and Tavernier reported seeing ghostly figures struggling in the waters between Conch and Crocker Reefs. As the sea phantoms were usually seen around the beginning of July, those who saw them took them to be from the stricken Spanish merchantman. This of course has not deterred the treasure-seekers who continually dive off Plantation Key. Artifacts from the wreck are to be found in the Museum of Sunken Treasure on Plantation Key.

A Triptych of Doomed Ships

From the archives of the American Merchant Marine three doomed American ships, the *Seabird*, the *Ellen Austin* and the *Abbey S Hart* stand out as victims of evil. To the superstitious these ships were assaulted by unseen hexing hands attracted by the American equivalent of the *Flying Dutchman* story.

In 1880, a seaman was standing on Easton's Beach, near Newport, Rhode Island, when he saw a ship under full sail on the horizon. His horror was not aroused just then, not until he realised as the ship came closer that it was heading straight for the beach and was making no signs of changing the crash course. Within minutes, the vessel, her canvas straining and hull grounding, ploughed up the sandy shore and came to a stop on an even keel.

The ship was recognised by her name as the *Seabird*, due to arrive that day in Newport, from Honduras. No-one appeared to answer the calls of the fishermen now assembled on the sand, so they climbed aboard. On the galley stove coffee was still boiling and a table was laid for breakfast. The ship was in good order; instruments and charts showed a correct course, and there was nothing in the log to indicate anything wrong. But there was no trace of the crew, nor any clue to reveal where they had gone or why. The only living creature on board was a terrified mongrel dog. To this day no-one knows what happened aboard the *Seabird*, but her course was held so skilfully that the superstitious believe that she *must* have been guided ashore by ghostly hands.

The second strange sea phantom story concerns the American clipper *Ellen Austin*, trading between New York and Liverpool, England. In the autumn of 1881 she was some 600 miles off the coast of Ireland when her lookout reported: 'Schooner on the port bow'. The captain of the *Ellen Austin* inspected the ship through his telescope and identified her as a large schooner under fore and main sails and jib. But no answer came from the mystery schooner when she was hailed. From the *Ellen Austin* there seemed to be no-one on the strange ship's deck.

Fearing that there might be plague aboard, the master of the *Ellen Austin* sent his medical orderlies aboard the strange ship to investigate. On their return they reported that the ship was entirely deserted and that there were signs aboard that she had been so for several months. Making the schooner fast, the captain of the *Ellen Austin* made plans for a salvage crew to board her and make her seaworthy. It was his plan to haul her back to New York and claim the salvage money for her.

Volunteers were asked for, but the crew of the *Ellen Austin* were wary of boarding the mystery ship. So the captain offered an extra bonus to all who would sail the schooner home. Thus were the men's superstitious fears overcome and a salvage crew took over the schooner. Next day a storm blew up and raged for several days; both ships battled along together until, some 300 miles off Sandy Hook, New Jersey, the weather calmed and the captain of the *Ellen Austin* hailed his prize. There was no answer. Filled with fear, a mate and several crewmen rowed to the schooner; but soon they were back on the *Ellen Austin* to report that the salvage crew had vanished.

The captain refused to believe their story and went aboard the schooner which he had searched from stem to stern. Nothing unusual was found and once more the captain ordered a salvage crew to take possession of the ship. This time they were to mount a constant guard and to hail the *Ellen Austin* should anything unusual happen. The next morning, the schooner was gone. Although he searched the sea around for several days the captain of the *Ellen Austin* found nothing, and his enquiries, once he gained New York, were fruitless. The mystery schooner had disappeared from the sea.

The crew of the *Ellen Austin*, of course, were convinced that the strange ship had been in the power of the supernatural. Certainly no logical explanation was ever found to account for her disappearance.

Such was the fate of the full-rigged American ship met by the Hamburg steamer *Pickhuben* in the Indian Ocean in September 1894. As the ship was approached, the master of the German vessel read her name, *Abbey S Hart*. On seeing no sign of life, volunteers from the *Pickhuben* went aboard. Below they found the crew all dead in their cabins, except the captain who was alive, but raving mad.

The *Abbey S Hart* was towed to Table Bay, Cape of Good Hope, by the *Pickhuben*. Examination of the ill-fated vessel and her log revealed that her last port of call had been Tanjong Piok, Java, for a cargo of sugar. Once again sea phantoms had struck, as they had the *Curang Medan* in 1948.

Chapter 5

Some Ghosts of the Pacific

Certain parts of the Pacific Ocean have earned the reputation of being haunted. The Pacific sea phantoms, however, are in a class by themselves, for they are said to be bent on the destruction of all shipping which strays across their territory. Down the centuries, whole argosies have disappeared in Pacific waters; there are even cases of rescue ships meeting with unaccountable fates, while out looking for missing vessels.

The Mystery of the Asiatic Prince

One famous haunted area is around the islands and reefs which make up the modern state of Hawaii and is the setting of one of the world's famous sea mysteries.

At 4 pm on March 16 1928 a pilot came aboard the *Asiatic Prince* in Los Angeles harbour. As the pilot installed himself on the bridge, ready to bark orders to the steersman, the 48-man crew, including 26 Chinese, were making the ship ready. From the bridge the pilot watched the seamen scuttle about their duties. The chief engineer was tanking the ship up to full capacity with 1,300 tons of fuel oil, and the mate was inspecting the emergency equipment and the four steel life-boats. At last all was pronounced ready.

It was the first time that the ship, flying British colours at her stern and the 'P' pennant of the International Code at her foremast, had put into Los Angeles harbour and it was to be her last accountable voyage. For, as the *Asiatic Prince* steamed for Yokohama, the hand of fate had enrolled her among the invisible flotilla whose shadowy wakes have been lost forever in the Pacific.

Out of Los Angeles the pilot left the ship and the Chadburn tinkled to 'Full Speed Ahead'. As the massive bows of the *Asiatic Prince*, now safely heading for Yokohama, braced to the swell, the captain recalled for a few moments the scandal his ship had caused in Britain.

With her speed of fifteen knots and burthen of 10,000 tons, the *Asiatic Prince* was well enough designed and built to do honour to the British Merchant Navy. But *Asiatic Prince* had set sail under a cloud. The fact was that she had been built in Germany, not England. All Britain had been indignant that the order for the ship's construction had gone to the Hamburg shipyards of the *Deutsche Werft*. At the time, Britain's economy was still struggling under the economic burdens brought on by World War I, money was short, unemployment was high and the loss of the *Asiatic Prince* had condemned numbers of skilled workmen to enforced idleness.

The owner of the *Asiatic Prince*, however, was quite explicit in his reasons for awarding the contract to the Germans. In his press statement he explained: 'I requested tenders, in the ordinary way, from several shipyards. That submitted by the *Deutsche Werft* was the cheapest. The Government should allow British industry to pay reasonable prices for the work it orders. That's not my affair, but theirs.'

As far as the proprietary Rio Cap Line were concerned, therefore, the matter was closed; but their ship had been publicly cursed and to the superstitious that was highly significant in view of the vessel's subsequent fate.

On his bridge, the captain smiled at the superstitious nonsense the uninformed had gabbled at him, and the warnings he had received not to sail the now 'doomed' ship. Already the *Asiatic Prince* was confounding her detractors. She had just crossed the Atlantic at an average speed of over 14 knots, despite bad weather. After calling at Norfolk, Colon, Panama and Los Angeles, where she had been much admired, the ship was about to tackle the Pacific and ultimately woo the shipbuilders of Yokohama.

When he had left the bridge the pilot had wished the captain good luck. But at that time the words seemed superfluous. All was well. The officer on duty had charted the winter route to Yokohama advised by the company. Indeed such voyages were practically automatic!

On April 6 1928, the British steamer *City of Eastbourne* cast anchor, five days late, in the roadstead of Yokohama. To the authorities at the Japanese port the skipper described how they had been held up by bad weather north of Hawaii. Apparently he had picked up an SOS from the tanker *British Hussar*, but could not locate her position.

Puzzled, the Japanese authorities consulted their files. On March 26 1928, the *Niagara* had also picked up an SOS from the *British Hussar*, but the *Niagara* officers had not been able to understand the geographical data given. The ship *Ventura* and several of the stations along the Nansei Shotô (Ryukyu Islands) and Izu Shichitô (along the coast of Japan's main island of Honchu) had also picked up the SOS messages. From these reports the *British Hussar* was thought to have been some 400 miles south-west of Hawaii.

Guided by this somewhat vague data, the American Navy despatched two destroyers, the *Burnus* and the *Ludlow*, from Pearl Harbour to take up the search. Both methodically searched the area for the British tanker for five days, but she had completely vanished. Experts believed that the *British Hussar* had broken in half. Because of their excessive length and weight of cargo, tankers were liable to this kind of accident in stormy weather. So the bad news was cabled to her owners.

The owners were puzzled by the cable, for as the *Burnus* and *Ludlow* searched the Pacific for the *British Hussar* she was safely moored off a landing stage at Abadan in the Persian Gulf! The captain of the *British Hussar* quickly confirmed to the owners that his ship had been nowhere near the Pacific during April 1928. The whole matter was found incomprehensible.

Nevertheless the reported SOS signals from the *British Hussar* had been no illusion. Several vessels and landward stations had received them. But the evidence stared them in the face, the *British Hussar* had not been in the Pacific at the time of transmission.

The British consul at Yokohama also tried to obtain further information. He found that four ships had been in the area of Hawaii when the ghost messages had been sent out; the *City of Eastbourne*, the *Niagara*, the *Ventura* and the *Asiatic Prince*—that was curious?—*Asiatic Prince* was also missing!

Enquiries were made at Tokyo, Kobe, Osaka and Nagasaki, even the major ports on the China coast were contacted, but to no avail. Under the date April 20 1928, the British consul officially recorded: '*Asiatic Prince* has simply vanished.'

In offices at Los Angeles, Yokohama, London and Abadan, however, the mystery was studied afresh:

The facts:

Between March 20-30 1928 that area of the Pacific, bounded by the quadrilateral made by the 20th and 35th parallels north and the 170th and 150th meridians east, had been the scene of two mysteries.

1. SOS from the *British Hussar*—no ship found—vessel actually 6,000 miles away.

2. *Asiatic Prince*—modern vessel with all the latest wireless equipment and life-boats completely vanished.

Both ships apparently very near each other according to the radio-goniometric data.

Wind exceeding Force No 12 of the Beaufort Scale (the highest figure recorded for wind strength, hurricane force).

Action taken:

The reports of the *City of Eastbourne*, *Niagara*, *Ventura*, *Ludlow* and *Burnus*, collated and re-checked.

Conclusion:

It is thought conceivable that the SOS signal reportedly sent out by the *British Hussar* was in fact transmitted by the *Asiatic Prince*. The question, 'If the above be true, why did *Asiatic Prince* transmit under the name *British Hussar*?' is thought to be resolved as follows.

The call sign received by operators was GJVR—ie, *British Hussar*. But the *Asiatic Prince's* call sign was GJVP—only one letter of difference. In morse P is .--., and R is .-.

Thus it is concluded that the central dash of the morse R was sent twice, thus leading to the confusion between the *British Hussar* and the *Asiatic Prince*. After which, the *Asiatic Prince* must have been caught in a hurricane, disabled and sunk with all hands.

The most curious fact, however, was how the 10,000 ton *Asiatic Prince* with new hull, new engines and new equipment could have sunk within a few seconds. For this she must have done, if her wireless equipment only sent out a brief message followed by complete silence!

The Rio Cap Line officially posted *Asiatic Prince* missing at Lloyd's in 1928; the official reason for loss was given as 'sunk off Hawaii during the storm of March [1928]'. Today the true reasons for the vessel's loss remain obscure. Many have put forward explanations for the fate of the *Asiatic Prince*, ranging from boiler explosions to Chinese pirates, but those who live around the Hawaiian islands believe they know what happened to her. The ghosts of the dead Pacific mariners, they say, had taken possession of the vessel which now glides through the island shadows on an endless voyage!

The Five-masted Copenhagen

In July 1930 an Argentine trading vessel was labouring in a fierce Pacific gale, and aboard it was all hands on deck in case of an emergency. It was during a lull in the lashing of the waves when most of the crew saw the phantom ship.

It appeared about a point off the port bow and was quite distinct even though the sighting only lasted a few seconds. Less than a mile away a phantom sailing vessel was seen scudding before the wind—a ship of enormous size with five masts, and canvas fully set. Her black hull had been clearly seen flecked by the storm's lightning flashes which had run the full length of her southwest pointed bows.

For a while the many members of the crew who had seen the phantom watched in silence, hardly believing what they had seen. They simply stared in the direction in which the phantom had disappeared. The lightning still flashed, but it now illuminated an empty sea.

When the storm abated, the captain of the Argentine steamer gathered the eye-witness accounts of the sighting, assuming personally that his crew must have been mistaken: for at that time there was no such thing as a five-master in any fleet in the world!

Five-master! Five-master! . . . the words persistently nagged at the captain's mind while he was at work in his cabin and even obtruded into his subconscious when he slept. At length a question posed itself: had the crew in fact seen the wraith of the *Copenhagen*?

Commanded by Captain Andersen, the 368′ 9″ long five-masted *Köbenhavn* (*Copenhagen* in English) had been built in 1924 for the Danish East Asiatic Company by Ramage & Ferguson of Leith, Scotland. The biggest sailing ship in the world, she was used exclusively for the training of future officers for the Danish Navy. For four years she had gracefully cut the waves between Great Britain and Thailand, Australia and Chile. On December 14 1928, however, she had set out to sea from Buenos Aires with a crew and 60 cadets aboard bound for Australia, by way of the Cape of Good Hope.

Although she was fitted out with all the up-to-date equipment including high-powered radio, the *Copenhagen* sent few messages, for her voyage presented a minimum of difficulties. Indeed her silence was to be expected. On December 22 1928, however, she signalled her position some 900 miles off Tristan da Cunha, adding that all was well on board and that the Danish lads were looking forward to Christmas as they rounded the Cape of Good Hope and entered the southern part of the Indian Ocean.

Alas, their happy voyage past the Crozet Isles and north of Amsterdam Island was not to take place. On March 22 1929, the International Press Agency lines buzzed with this message:

'MORE THAN 100 DAYS SINCE LAST NEWS OF
COPENHAGEN—LEFT ARGENTINA FOR
AUSTRALIA WITH 75 ON BOARD—MUCH
UNEASINESS FELT AS TO FATE OF VESSEL—
EQUIPPED WITH WIRELESS AND AUXILIARY
ENGINES'

In Denmark no-one really worried. *Copenhagen* had been silent before. She had once remained at sea for eighty days without giving any sign of life! As the months passed with no word from *Copenhagen*, complacency turned to apprehension in Denmark. What had caused this extended silence?

No SOS messages or signals of distress of any kind were received from *Copenhagen*, but the directors of the Danish East Asiatic Company decided to make some investigations. The motorship *Mexico* was despatched to Tristan da Cunha.

Tristan da Cunha is an island midway between South Africa and South America. The loneliest island in the world, it arose from obscurity in 1506 on discovery by the Portuguese. A military force was stationed at Tristan while Napoleon was imprisoned at St Helena, and many of the soldiers' descendants remained. In the 1930s, Tristan's recorded population numbered under 200, many of whom were fishermen. Had any of them seen any signs of the *Copenhagen*?

One fisherman testified that he had seen a large sailing ship. His story was corroborated by others. The fisherman and his mates were not sure that the ship had had five masts, all they remembered was that the foremast was broken. The ship did not fly distress signals and eventually was seen to sail away from Tristan, although she made no attempt to contact or put into the island. No wreckage purporting to be from the *Copenhagen* was found.

For ten days the *Mexico* searched the sea from Tristan to Cape Town; nothing was found. On September 11 1929 the Danish newspapers *Kristeligt Dagblad, Berlingske Aftenavis* and *Bonsen* (Denmark's Commercial and Shipping Daily) carried the official report that *Copenhagen* was regarded as lost at sea in a storm.

Copenhagen was almost forgotten until fishermen off the coast of Chile began to report sighting a five-masted sailing ship. Then in July 1930 the aforementioned Argentine vessel made a sighting. The following month a coaster also sighted *Copenhagen*, this time off Easter Island. Three weeks later, the passengers on board a small liner reported seeing a phantom five-master off the Peruvian coast. Each person who made a sighting was carefully examined. All the accounts agreed. Fraud was ruled out. While the investigations were underway, some wreckage was picked up off the west coast of Australia; on one fragment of stern was the distinct lettering KÖBENHAVN.

In December 1938, a trawler brought into Cape Town a bottle which had been found in the fishnets while fishing some forty miles southeast of the South African capital. Inside the bottle was a scrap of paper written in very bad English. Most of the words were incomprehensible but what could be made out was the position 47 deg 37' south and 02 deg 14' and 'Easterly wind . . . icebergs . . . surrounded', and the name KÖBENHAVN.

The position mentioned was duly charted and found to be some 625 miles southwest of Tristan da Cunha. Thus was the fate of the *Copenhagen* officially logged, but hundreds of miles away from where she was deemed wrecked, her spectre continued to ply her eternal voyage.

Chapter 6

Ghost Ships
of the Goodwin Sands

At low tide, ball games can be played on parts of the notorious Goodwin Sands which lie on the steep eastern edge of an uneven submarine platform of chalk some six miles east of the town of Deal, Kent. The Sands are some 11 miles long, by four miles across, and are covered with an average of 12 feet of water at high tide. Other parts form very treacherous quicksands which have ingested whole many a trapped vessel. For nearly a thousand years men have speculated upon and feared the Goodwin Sands, its knolls and ridges, channels and scourpits with their characteristic fan-shapes of current-built shoals. Its first mention as the 'Island of Lomea' (*Insula Lomea*) is to be found in a chronicle, *De Rebus Albionicis Britannicus* (1590), written by the schoolmaster-antiquary-member of parliament John Twyne (1501-81), who noted:

'. . . this isle was very fruitful and had much pasture; it was situated lower than Thanet from which there was a passage by boat of about three or four miles. This Island in an unusual tempest of winds and rain and in a very high rage of the sea was drowned, overwhelmed with sand, and irrecoverably converted into a nature between that of land and sea . . . sometimes it floats, while at low water, people may walk upon it.'

Thereafter, such chroniclers as the famous antiquary William Camden (1551-1623), in his *Britannia* (1586), and the father of English topography William Lambarde in his *Perambulation of Kent* (1576), perpetuated an aura of the sinister and ominous when mentioning the Goodwin Sands.

Eventually the whole area was nicknamed 'the shippe swalower' (*navium gurges et vorago*).

William Shakespeare knew of the dreaded Goodwin Sands. In his *Merchant of Venice*, the character Salarino speaks of the merchant Antonio having 'a ship of rich lading wracked on the narrow seas; the Goodwins, I think they call the place; a very dangerous flat, and fatal, where the carcasses of many a tall ship lie buried'. By Shakespeare's time, of course, the legend that *Insula Lomea* once formed a part of the estate owned by Godwine, Earl of Wessex, adviser to King Cnut, was well established.

With its bodeful past it is not surprising that the Goodwin Sands have been populated with ghosts in local legends, which are the favourite talking points among the many public house gossips of Deal and Walmer.

The earliest chart which shows the Goodwins, on a scale sufficiently large for navigation, is to be found in a 1588 edition of *The Mariner's Mirror* drawn by Dutchman Lucas J. Waghenaar. The tales of ghost ships hereabouts, however, date from later wrecks and storms.

November 1753

Some unauthenticated stories tell how such stricken vessels as the 60-gun *Shrewsbury* lost in 1703, and the screw steamer *Sorrento* which sank in 1872, appear on the anniversaries of their disasters. Other tales are more authoritative, and among them is that recorded by Richard Hakluyt (1553-1616), the first of the English geographers. According to Hakluyt, as the Spanish Armada, commanded by Alonso Perez de Guzmán el Bueno, Duke of Medina Sidonia, was being routed in the 'Battle of the Narrow Seas' (July 29-August 9 1588) by the vessels of Lord Howard of Effingham, one conspicuously strange event occurred.

On board one leading galleon a captain prepared to

surrender to an approaching English ship. Angered by this, a junior officer slew the captain, only to be cut down himself seconds later by the captain's brother. As the ship's officers fought amongst themselves, the galleon, aflame from stem to stern, was driven hard onto the Goodwins. With her guns firing distress signals, the galleon soon broke up and her crew were drowned. This incident was considered responsible for a supernatural occurrence over a 100 years later.

Throughout the night of November 25-26 1703, England was lashed by the worst storms in meteorological history. Out at sea a squadron of thirteen ships of the Royal Navy, returning to Chatham, fought hard for shelter and approached the Goodwin Sands. One by one the ships went to their doom around the Thames estuary, but the Sands claimed four frigates; the *Northumberland* (commanded by James Greenway, with a crew of 253), the *Restoration* (under Captain Fleetwood Emes, with a crew of 368), the *Stirling Castle* (with Commander Johnson and 349 men aboard) and the *Mary* (carrying Rear Admiral Beaumont and a crew of 273).

Out of all the hundreds of men lost on the Goodwins that night, only two seamen, from the *Mary*, survived and later offered this curious testimony:

'A great warship of Drake's day, her sails tattered, burning from fore to aft and her guns firing, served by demented seamen, bore down on us, sailed right through our ship and finally disappeared before our eyes into the depths of the Sands.'

Strangely enough, the captain of a big East India clipper, inward bound for London, saw the spectre of the *Mary's* companion frigate the *Northumberland*. He recorded in his log:

'*November* 28 1753: At ten of the clock this day, while riding out bad weather off [the] Goodwins, awaiting better conditions to continue our passage, an armed frigate came driving down on my ship, her masts gone, her decks and hull in fearful shape. It seemed to us all there could be no avoiding her coming athwart our anchor-chains with dire results, and I was about to order my first officer to slip our anchors when we made out the frigate for what she was. Her name became clear for all to read; it was *Northumberland*, and as she came on, sweeping down on my ship, we saw men running in panic about her main deck. She appeared to be unmanageable. We watched in horror, for the wind was not strong enough to place any ship in such condition, and then it pleased Almighty God the phantom, for such it surely was, steered contrary to our mounting anxieties to windward and so drove on clear of us, but no more than two ships' lengths to our leeward, and so disappeared in what seemed a dark haze. It was a spectacle far too terrible to dwell upon, to see this ghost of what was once a fine warship going to her doom a second time. We saw a little steady trickle of men leaping into the sea, one after another, but their bodies made no splash as they struck the waters. The cries of her spectral crew, the firing of her guns every half-minute for assistance, filled us all with dread and terror that my men, as I, were nigh dead with the horror of it all.'[1]

The Loss of the Violet

One of the most appalling Goodwin Sands incidents, however, was the total loss, with all hands and passengers, of the mail steamer *Violet*, bound from Ostend to Dover.

It was on a night of driving snow squalls in the year 1857. Although the moon, scudding through clouds, only briefly lit the choppy sea, the North Sand Head lightship spotted the *Violet* on a crash course with the Goodwin Sands. A moment later the *Violet* had struck the Sands in a smother of surf and at once fired her rockets and signal cannons.

---

[1]See: Armstrong, Warren. *Sea Phantoms*. (Odhams Press, London, 1964), p 45.

Three hours later the Ramsgate tug *Aid* arrived on the scene, with a lifeboat in tow. Even though the Sands were thoroughly searched, nothing whatsoever could be found of the *Violet* and her crew. Staying in the area until daybreak the lifeboatmen and their helpers searched again. This time they found a mast sticking out of the water and, wallowing in the flood-tide, a lifebuoy painted with the words *SS Violet* to which three battered bodies were lashed. According to Lloyd's, her mail was recovered on January 6 1857.

On January 1 1947, George Goldsmith Carter was on the North Goodwin lightship and recorded this curious incident concerning the *Violet*:

'We saw a steamer approaching the Goodwins, heading straight for them as the foredoomed *Violet* must have done, and vanishing in a squall of driving snow. When the snow had passed we saw rockets, pale and feeble over the Goodwins. We fired answering rockets and radioed the shore. Not long afterwards the Ramsgate lifeboat arrived and we directed them to where we had seen the rockets.'[2]

Some hours later the Ramsgate lifeboat returned alongside the North Sand Head lightship. The coxswain reported grimly that he could not find anything. Aboard the lightship, however, all who had sighted the steamer were convinced that it was the wraith of the *Violet* they had seen, ninety years on!

The Wreck of the Lady Luvibond

The wreck of the *Lady Luvibond* is another persistent Goodwin Sands ghost story. During the evening of February 13 1748, the schooner *Lady Luvibond*, loaded with a general cargo for Oporto, and under the command of Captain Simon Reed, sailed down the Thames to safely clear the

---

[2]For G. G. Carter's personal testimony see: *The Goodwin Sands*. (Constable, London, 1953), pp 137-8.

North Foreland. Captain Reed was particularly happy on this trip, for he had his new wife aboard along with her mother and their wedding guests. On deck, however, while the guests were drinking toasts to the newly married couple in the captain's cabin below, first mate John Rivers, who had been a rival for the affections of Simon Reed's wife, nursed his hatred and jealousy.

A fair wind blew that night and the *Lady Luvibond* sped across the water. But, as he stood in the wind, something must have snapped in John Rivers' mind. He walked casually aft and drew a heavy wooden belaying-pin from a rack. Deliberately he strolled towards the helmsman and, pretending to peer over the man's shoulder at the binnacle, Rivers shattered the poor sailor's skull with the belaying-pin. Rolling the lifeless body into the scuppers, Rivers took the helm and swung the *Lady Luvibond* hard over.

In the captain's cabin the bridal party still made merry, too preoccupied to notice the ship's change of course, until, with a grinding crash, the schooner hit the Goodwin Sands. The masts snapped and toppled into the sea, and the timbers rent like matchwood with earsplitting groans. Down in the cabin the captain and his guests were trapped and helpless. Above the din of the dying ship rose the hideous cacophony of Rivers' revengeful laughter.

By first light on February 14 1748, the *Lady Luvibond* had been sucked into the Goodwin Sands for ever. At the subsequent court of enquiry John Rivers' mother gave evidence that she had 'heard her son say he would get even with Simon Reed if it cost him his life.' The case of the *Lady Luvibond* was logged as wrecked by misadventure.

Fifty years later to the day, Captain James Westlake, aboard the coasting vessel *Edenbridge*, was skirting the edge of the Goodwin Sands, when he caught sight of a three-masted schooner bearing down on him with sails set. Shouting to the helmsman to slam the *Edenbridge's* wheel hard over, Westlake watched the other craft sheer past.

As it did so, Westlake heard the sound of female voices and merrymaking coming from the ship's lower deck.

Reporting the incident to his ship's owners, Westlake discovered that the crew of a fishing vessel had seen the same schooner go ashore on the Goodwins, to break up before their eyes. Making to rescue any survivors, the crew of the fishing vessel found nothing but empty sand and water. The *Lady Luvibond* had made her first phantom appearance.

On February 13 1848, Deal hovellers watched the spectral *Lady Luvibond* go aground once again. They too set out to the rescue but found nothing. Again on February 13 1898, shore watchers saw the *Lady Luvibond* re-enact her pile-up on the Goodwin Sands. They launched off, but found no trace of the wreck.

Other ships at sea have seen the *Lady Luvibond* go aground, and, during early January 1948, the 2,327 ton Italian vessel *Silvia Onorato* was wrecked on the Goodwins. Some said that this time the *Lady Luvibond* had demanded a live sacrifice for her anniversary.

Consistently, the locals point out, every 50 years, on the exact anniversary of her doom, the phantom *Lady Luvibond* has re-enacted the consequences of a madman's deed of violence. No doubt on February 13 1998, on the 250th anniversary of her wrecking, researchers with the sophisticated equipment for ghosthunting which might have been developed by then, will set out for a sight of this ghost ship, this time to put her appearance on visual record.

Many strange sounds are still borne on the wind from the yeasty smother of the southward Goodwin Sands. 'Gull cries' say the sceptical. But those who live thereabouts know that no gull hatched on the seven seas ever made such a noise. Only the moans of the waking dead devoured by the Goodwins, the old folk aver, could ever utter such heart-rending and forlorn cries!

Chapter 7

The Mystery of the *Affray*

Laid down January 16 1944 and launched April 12 1945, HMS *Affray* was completed May 2 1946. A British Class A submarine, she was of 1,500 tons displacement.

At 4.15 pm on April 16 1951, the *Affray* sailed from Portsmouth naval base for a training cruise of the Western Approaches. On board was her normal complement of crew along with officers in training, an instructor and some Royal Marine commandos—a total of 75. She steered a course south of the Isle of Wight and proceeded at a steady 4½ knots for Falmouth, where she was scheduled to surface around 8.30 am. Shortly after 9.00 pm on the evening of her departure, *Affray* signalled that she was about to submerge. From that moment until June 14 1951 her exact location was a complete mystery! *Affray* had been due to surface and make a signal by 9.00 am on the morning of April 17. When no signal was received, however, 'Operation Subsunk' was set in motion on a massive scale.

The search ships of several nations joined British vessels to scour the Channel, and aircraft from the Fleet Air Arm and the RAF zigzagged across the sea from the English to the French coast. It was all to no avail. On the evening of April 19 the operation was called off and the newspaper headlines spelt out to the nation that there could be no hope of survivors among the 75 on board.

By April 18 the Admiralty had issued an official statement:

'1. The submarine *Affray* has not surfaced as expected after diving while on exercise. She sailed from Portsmouth unescorted and dived at 2115 hours south of the Isle of Wight. She was proceeding westward submerged at a speed of 4½ knots.

'2. She was expected to surface at 0830 this morning but no surfacing signal has been received and her present position is unknown. Naval craft including helicopters have been alerted and begun search and five destroyers have put to sea. Every attempt is being made to contact the submarine by radio.

'3. The following message is being broadcast hourly to shipping: "Submarine missing, possibly sunk between positions 50° 10′ N, 1° 45′ W, 49° 40′ N, 4° W. Vessels in the vicinity are requested to keep sharp lookout for survivors and to report wreckage, oil slicks on the surface or any other indications to the Commander in Chief, Portsmouth".

'4. Vessels engaged in the search include six submarines, two United States destroyers, six frigates, six destroyers, various aircraft and helicopters.

'5. The weather forecast is quite good. It is neap tides, which means that the rise and fall of the tide is the minimum.

'6. The *Affray* was carrying out a war patrol and was due to make Falmouth; this means that on passage she would have been continually submerged and at times at considerable depth. In her orders she was, however, required to report herself hourly. No such report has been received. She may be proceeding submerged, having misread her orders for these regular reports. If in so doing she is carrying out a deep diving patrol she would not be able to pick up messages which are being made to her every fifteen minutes by Rugby radio station.

'7. In view of the lapse of time the chances of the submarine having misinterpreted her instructions are lessening and the chances of an accident must be regarded as increasingly probable.'

Because the *Affray* could be lying anywhere within an area of several thousand square miles, owing to the latitude of the instructions given to the submarine's commander, the search for wreckage of the *Affray* was a colossal and difficult task. Moreover, the area was strewn with the wrecks of two world wars as well as many peacetime sinkings.

It was the task of Admiralty Salvage Vessel *HMS Reclaim* to follow up the searching force to identify the 250 or so wrecks located. Altogether it was a slow and arduous progress because of the strong tides and the great depth of water on the French side of the Channel.

Eventually, Admiralty scientists at the Teddington Research Laboratory produced an underwater television set that could be connected to a viewing screen on the *Reclaim*. Around noon on June 14 1951, the *Reclaim* was investigating a wreck located on the edge of Hurd Deep (about 15 miles north-west of the Casquets) when the underwater television camera picked up the outline of a nameplate. The camera was fixed on the nameplate and made to scan the letters A-F-F-R-A-Y and the long search for the missing submarine was over.

Affray, apparently from her location, had travelled safely submerged for some eight hours from the moment she had signalled 'Am diving'; a distance of almost 40 miles. Now, she lay on the bottom of the sea less than a dozen miles due north of Alderney, in the Channel Islands, with a list to port of about 15 degrees.

Her hydroplanes were at hard rise (ie, to surface the submarine), the indicator buoys (red and yellow markers which would light up at night) had not been released and the only sign of damage was to the long snort mast, which had broken away except for a thin sliver of metal. Her tubular mast lay over the port ballast tanks, with its head resting on the seabed. The upper 28 feet of the mast was recovered and the welding was found to be faulty.

It was not possible to discover much else about the *Affray* as she was never raised: the *precise* cause of the disaster is still unknown. Several experts advanced the idea that the entire crew was killed by some sudden explosion, but this could never be proved. The superstitious, however, had a different explanation.

Warren Armstrong recorded[1] 12 years after the *Affray* disaster that he had met with the wife of a British rear admiral who gave him this startling testimony. Apparently she was about to retire to bed for the night when:

'Quite suddenly, I realised I was not alone in my room and in the half light I recognised my visitor. He had been serving as an engineer officer in my husband's ship, a cruiser, at a time when my husband was engineer-commander, and we had often entertained him in our Channel Islands home.

'He approached me and then stood still and silent; I was astonished to see him dressed in normal submariner's uniform although I did not recognise this fact until later when I described his clothing to my husband. Then he spoke quite clearly and said: "Tell your husband we are at the north end of Hurd Deep, nearly 70 miles from the lighthouse at St Catherine's Point. It happened very suddenly and none of us expected it." After that the speaker vanished.

'I immediately spoke to my husband by telephone, for he was then in a shore appointment in England, and to my dismay he told me, first, that he was not aware that this young officer was even in the *Affray*, nor that he had volunteered for the submarine service. It was all very puzzling. We spoke again by telephone to each other a few days later, when my husband told me that the search was being carried out in quite a different part of the Channel from where my visitor had indicated to me—and, as you know, wrongly, as it turned out later. This being so, my husband said, there did not seem to be anything he could do about it.'

Once again a phantom from the deep had materialised to reveal the secrets of a maritime tragedy. Nothing could be done, however, in this case, for few if any would have believed the rear admiral's wife's story, for such is man's understanding of the realm of ghosts.

---

[1] *Sea phantoms*, pp 158-59.

Chapter 8

Voices from the Sea

Many who have walked along the seashore at dusk have strongly believed that some of the sounds they heard coming from the sea were far too eerie to be dismissed as the lapping of water, or the cries of seagulls. Countless seamen, for instance, say they have heard ghostly voices coming from the trough of waves off the shore near Southwold in Suffolk. In his *Mardles From Suffolk*, Ernest Cooper quotes an old Southwold pilot on the subject:

'I well recollect one time when I was in the cutter, I had the watch alone one night, and stood still at the tiller looking around, but there was nothing in sight except a steamboat or two miles away. When all of a sudden I heard someone sing out "Ship Ahoy", on our port quarter, and I looked but I couldn't see any craft anywhere. Then I heard it again right plain "Ship Ahoy", and I shoved the tiller down and runned to the companion-way and hollared down: "Here tumble up quick, here's some poor devil afloat." Up they come and launched the boat as quick as possible; they pulled round and I kept torching for an hour or more, but we never see or heard anything, and I can't tell ye now whether that's a man or someone from Fiddler's Green, you know, where the drowned sailors go.'

Yorkshire Jack

Another voice, that of a sailor called Yorkshire Jack, can still be heard, many fishermen testify, in Mounts Bay, off the coast of Cornwall.

During the early 1800s there lived in the village of Ludgvan, near Penzance, an old man called Polgrain and his young wife Sarah. Having long lost whatever love she had had for her elderly husband, Sarah Polgrain took up with a sailor of her own age known locally as Yorkshire Jack. Sarah's quarrels with her husband thereafter became a daily occurrence, and the neighbours were soon accustomed to the sounds of furniture crashing as Sarah berated her husband.

One morning, however, Sarah came running into her neighbour's cottage very agitated and pale. She believed that her husband had suddenly been seized by cholera and was very ill. Later she returned to the same neighbour with the news that her husband was dead. At the time no-one suspected anything wrong. The doctor, apparently, was satisfied that the death was due to cholera, and a certificate to that effect was given. Not long after the funeral, however, rumours of foul play began to circulate.

Public opinion became so agitated that the local authorities demanded a full enquiry. Mr Polgrain's body was exhumed, and on examination was found to contain enough arsenic to kill several people. Sarah Polgrain was arrested and charged with murder. The case against her was damning and she was found guilty and sentenced to be hanged.

On the day appointed for her public execution, Sarah Polgrain, as a last request, asked that Yorkshire Jack might be allowed to accompany her to the scaffold. The request was granted and Jack was even permitted to mount to the gallows platform. Just as the rope was placed around Sarah's neck, Jack kissed her and the two embraced for the last time. Spectators near the gallows then heard Sarah say in slow measured tones, 'You will?'. To which Jack replied nervously, 'I will'.

Not long after her execution, the ghost of Sarah Polgrain was seen twice around Ludgvan; once in the churchyard by a local resident and once by a stranger on the highroad between Penzance and Hayle. The one to be most disturbed by Sarah's ghost, however, was Yorkshire Jack.

After Sarah's execution, a marked change was noticed in the young sailor. Gone was his gaiety and abandonment, which had been replaced by sour-temper and moroseness. His once healthy complexion turned to a ghostly pallor and he developed the neurotic habit of constantly looking over his shoulder. In the comparative safety of the local inn's snug, he admitted to friends: 'She gives me no peace. Wherever I go she follows me. Wherever I turn, I find her at my elbow'. All guessed that the 'she' he constantly mentioned was the ghost of Sarah Polgrain.

Even though Jack went back to sea, the strange, uncanny presence followed him. His shipmates often saw him looking over his shoulder at something they couldn't see. But at night, when lying in their hammocks in the fo'c'sle, they too were constantly aware of a strange, unpleasant presence standing in their midst.

This went on for weeks and weeks, until their ship returned home, and they were in sight once more of Mounts Bay. Then one morning, Jack, more restless and morose than usual, confided in his assembled mates.

'When I was on the scaffold that morning talking to Sarah Polgrain,' he explained, 'she made me promise on my oath that on this very day, at midnight, I would marry her. Thinking to humour her, and supposing trouble to have unhinged her mind, I agreed. But I know now that she was quite sane and much in earnest. Not being able to wed me in the flesh, she means to bind me to her for ever in the spirit.'

The following night, close on twelve o'clock, the whole fo'c'sle was awakened by the sound of footsteps, made it seemed by someone wearing high-heeled shoes. The tap, tapping along the passage leading amidships stopped along-side Yorkshire Jack's hammock. Trembling, his features contorted with terror, Jack arose without uttering a sound, left the fo'c'sle and climbed back on deck. The tap, tapping went with him all the way.

Once on deck, Jack walked straight to the bulwarks.

Clambering on to them he leapt deliberately into the sea. Just for a moment or so, his shipmates, who had followed him, caught sight of two white faces amid the black billows of the sea, and then they were gone.

According to the statements of certain eye-witnesses, directly the faces had disappeared, there was heard the far away chiming of church bells. All believed they were Jack's wedding bells; at last Sarah had married him. Even up to the early 1900s, fishermen frequently reported hearing bells in Mounts Bay and the cries of a forlorn voice shouting 'I will, I will'.

Sailors lured to their doom by ghostly voices from the sea is a popular theme in traditional legend and mythology; the story of Scylla and Charybdis (*Odyssey* Bk XI, Ch II, lines 85-100), the references in Greek mythology to the Sirens, the sea-nymphs who could lure to destruction those who heard their songs, and the German *Lorelei* being perhaps the most famous. Some of the cases of lighthouse ghosts, however, are also connected with ghostly voices from the sea.

The Light on Eilean Mor

The Flannan Isles, or the Seven Hunters, lie at Lat 58° 17' north and Long 7° 35' west, out in the North Atlantic, some 20 miles off Gallan Head, Lewis, in the Outer Hebrides. Here, in this group of uninhabited islands, in December 1900, was enacted a mystery which is still considered a classic among the insoluble enigmas of the sea.

Called *Insulae Sacrae* by George Buchanan (1506-82), the celebrated Scottish humanist, historian and Latinist, the Flannans had long been considered a serious menace to shipping. As disaster followed disaster among ships bound for the Butt of Lewis, the Pentland Firth, or for Scandinavian and Baltic ports, it was decided to set up a lighthouse among the islands. In 1895, the responsibility for a light on Eilean Mor was taken by the Northern Lighthouse Board. Because of the difficulty of constructing a lighthouse here—often materials had to be unloaded midst raging seas—it was not completed until 1899:

'The Commissioners of Northern Lighthouses hereby give Notice, that on the night of Thursday of the 7th of December next, and every evening thereafter from the going away of daylight in the evening till the return of daylight in the morning, a Light will be exhibited from a Lighthouse which has been erected on Eilean Mor . . . The Light will be a Group Flashing White Light showing 2 flashes in quick succession every half minute. The power of the Light will be equal to about 140,000 standard candles. The Light will be visible all round and will be elevated 330 feet above high water spring tides, and allowing fifteen feet for the height of the eye will be seen at about 24 nautical miles in clear weather, and at lesser distances according to the state of the atmosphere. When close to, the stacks lying to the westward of Eilean Mor will obscure the Light over two small angles. The top of the Lantern is about 75 feet above the island.

By order of the Board
Edinburgh, 30th Oct., 1899   James Murdoch, Secretary'

On the night of December 15 1900, a small freighter, the *SS Archer* under Captain Holman, homeward bound for the port of Greenock, failed to pick up the light from Eilean Mor. Captain Holman reported this fact by morse to the shore station, and the date and time was later logged as the official beginning of the mystery.

Because of heavy weather, the relief ship *Hesperus*, under the command of Captain Harvey, was late in arriving off Eilean Mor with supplies, on December 26 1900. Also aboard *Hesperus* was lightkeeper Joseph Moore who was now returning to the island to relieve one of the three keepers still believed to be on duty at Eilean Mor. But, as *Hesperus* hove to off the east landing stage, none of the three keepers, James Ducat (chief keeper), Thomas Marshall (first assistant), and Donald McArthur (supernumerary) appeared.

In normal circumstances, the keeper to be relieved by Joseph Moore would have been waiting at the east landing place to help unload the usual mails and provisions, and then be transferred aboard *Hesperus* to the shore-station at Breascleit, on Loch Roag, Lewis. As no-one appeared, Moore hurried up the long zigzag staircase to the lighthouse to investigate. He found the living quarters and storerooms empty. The clock on the mantlepiece had ticked to a standstill, and the ashes in the fireplace were cold. Puzzled and concerned, Moore raced back to the landing stage to report to Captain Harvey.

Buoymaster Macdonald with seamen Lamont and Campbell disembarked and joined Moore in a thorough search of the lighthouse. They ransacked all the main buildings and outhouses, but found nothing of the three missing keepers. Then they scoured the cliffs, rocks and caverns of Eilean Mor, but again found nothing unusual. Even the landing place was precisely in order as it had been on the last supply trip of December 6 1900. What they did find, however, was that the *west* landing stage of the island had been subjected to severe buffeting by waves in the storm which had delayed the *Hesperus*. At the foot of the stone staircase of the landing stage the iron railings had been twisted, and by the crane platform, ropes and jibs had been dislodged. The oil-skins and seaboots belonging to the lightkeepers were also discovered to be missing.

On checking keeper Ducat's log, the last entries were found to be dated December 13, with confirmation that at the time of writing a furious gale was blowing. On a slate nearby was a note (for subsequent transfer to the log book), timed at 9.00 am and dated Saturday December 15 1900, concerning relevant barometric and thermometric readings. Nothing more. Thus, whenever the tragedy occurred it was *after* then. Captain Holman of the *SS Archer*, it will be remembered, reported that, as he passed the Seven Hunters at midnight on December 15-16 1900, he failed to see the light. Even though it is thus possible to fix with a degree of certainty the day of the haunting tragedy, and the hour between reasonable limits, the actual *cause and nature* of why and how the three lighthousekeepers came to be missing remains a mystery.

A full-scale official investigation was made with the finding that 'from traces evident of former bad weather conditions experienced in the area in the period ten days to the time of their disappearance, it must be concluded that the three men left their posts possibly to secure gear or to ascertain the exact extent of storm damage at the landing stage, and were there caught by an unexpectedly heavy sea and drowned.'

Many lighthousekeepers, however, did not accept this official statement. They found it untenable to believe that three tried and experienced keepers would *all* have willingly ventured out in such weather to such a perilous spot as the west landing stage on Eilean Mor. But only the superstitious could offer any other explanation. They averred that it was the 'voices' often heard in these parts which had lured the three keepers to their deaths.

Once, lobster-fishermen and trawlermen had been regular visitors to the waters round Eilean Mor and many had been drowned. It was said that the ghosts of those who had been drowned still called for help when the seas raged. So, the superstitious said, on the night of December 15 1900, the three keepers had been lured by these phantom voices calling for help and had met their deaths on the rocks of Eilean Mor. Wilfred Wilson Gibson in his *Collected Poems* 1905-1925 (Macmillan, London 1933, pp 171-74) immortalised the saga in his poem *Flannan Isle*:

'Aye, though we hunted high and low, and hunted every-
    where,
Of the three men's fate we found no trace,

Of any kind in any place
But a door ajar, and an untouch'd meal
And an overtoppled chair;
And as we listened in the gloom of that forsaken livingroom,
A chill clutch on our breath,
We thought how ill-chance came to all who kept the
    Flannan Light . . .
And long we thought of the three we sought—
And of what might yet befall!'

The Cries of Pollacharra

Certainly the superstition surrounding phantom voices in the sea is well established amongst the northern islands of Scotland. From the early collection of authenticated folk stories made by the Revd Fr Allan McDonald (d 1905) comes a further example of the voices[1]:

'Towards the end of 1890 cries of people as if drowning were heard from the shore at Pollacharra in the direction of Lingay Island in the South of Barra. So distinct were the cries that a boat proceeded immediately in the direction. One of [those] in the boat (Rory Morrison, [of] Smerclet) [a township in South Uist], gave me the narrative. After proceeding on their way for some time the crying and shouting ceased, and the men in the boat were thinking of turning back to shore and had actually turned round the boat when the shouting began again, and they speedily pulled round and hastened forward. After a short time the shouting ceased again and the men once more thought of returning, and as they were preparing to do so the shouting was renewed again and they went forward once more, but after doing their best to find anyone in distress, they were obliged to give up and go home. All the crew heard the shouts distinctly.

---

[1]'Cries Heard on the Sea' Notebook II, 60 as extracted by John Campbell and Trevor Hall in *Strange Things* (Routledge and Kegan Paul, London 1968) pp 274-75.

No one was lost at the spot at the time. The shouting is supposed to be a warning of something untoward going to happen at the spot in question.'

In October 1898, an Eriskay boat struck the rock at the very spot described by Rory Morrison and all the crew were nearly drowned.

The Troubled Souls of Glamorgan

Around the lonely coastline of Glamorgan, South Wales, between the mouth of the River Ogmore and Dunraven Castle, and on Tuskar Rock, just over a mile offshore from Ogmore itself, ghosts are said to howl and materialise just before the break-up of fine weather. The local residents around Glamorgan and the crews of ships passing to and from Cardiff have all testified to the principal manifestations.

Five main sea phantoms have been seen; two screaming boys endeavouring to clamber out of the reach of the waves; a young man, dressed in sailor's clothes of the days of Elizabeth I, is seen in the water shouting for help; a weeping girl dressed in white; a demented man running along the foreshore to disappear in the rain; and strangest of all, the apparition of a claw-like hand on the beach clasping and flexing its fingers to the accompaniment of a man's screams of agony.

These ghosts are thought to be bound up with the mysterious Lord of Dunraven. In the 1650s a Welsh pamphlet was published telling this lord's strange story. This is a transcript of the original Welsh:

'Walter, though some say George, Vaughan, was Lord of Dunraven; he was reputed to be an "ingenious" fellow, his great fault being inordinate vanity. Soon after he inherited his title and the family property, including Dunraven Castle, a ship was wrecked on the dangerous rocks near the castle. Taking a rope, Vaughan swam out to the vessel and by this brave deed saved the entire crew. The incident

Horatio Viscount Nelson, Duke of Brontë (1758-1805). He was superstitious enough to have a horseshoe attached to the main mast of his flagship *Victory*. (*National Portrait Gallery, London*.)

Admiral Sir Cloudesley Shovel (1650-1707). His death and the wrecking of his flagship *HMS Association* is believed to have been caused by the curse of a sailor unjustly condemned to death. (*National Portrait Gallery, London*.)

Often sea captains would visit magicians and astrologers to discover if their coming voyage would be well attended with good fortune. (*The Curators of the Bodleian Library.*)

Many a sailor and naval officer has consulted a witch to buy amulets and talismans for a lucky voyage. (*The Curators of the Bodleian Library.*)

Admiral Sir George Tryon KCB (1832-93). His wraith is said to have
appeared to his wife at the moment of his death. (*Author's Collection.*)

took such hold of his mind that he set himself to devise some means of saving lives in cases of shipwreck. His scheme was laid . . . before the government, but . . . was rejected. This slight, as Vaughan considered it, touched . . . his vanity, and his resentment was such that it is said it altered him completely . . . He decided he would revive the hospitalities of the Welsh chieftains of old, and thus would his name be known far and wide . . .

'The years passed, and his reckless prodigality soon [wasted] his fortune; his castle was almost deserted and his former friends all departed.

'His oldest son and heir, realising that his inheritance was gone, determined to seek his fortune in foreign lands; the father most reluctantly gave his consent to this desire, but the parting between him and his son was affecting and seemed to revive Vaughan's parental affection . . . His one thought now was how he could retrieve his fortune for his sons.

'A wreck occurring some days later served considerably to replenish his coffers, as property "cast up by the sea", it was said, had by right belonged to the lord of the manor from Saxon times. The jingling of gold coins, unexpectedly come into Vaughan's possession . . . unhinged [his] mind [to consider] the possibility of making even more money by means of wrecking. For the furtherance of his scheme, Vaughan sought the help and advice of a man of desperate habits living in the neighbourhood, known as "Matt-of-the-Iron-Hand". This wretch had been captain of a pirate ship many years before and, on one occasion, the vessel had been seized by order of Vaughan, then a magistrate. In the taking of this ship a desperate struggle had ensued during which the captain lost one hand, afterward replaced by an iron hook fastened to the stump of the wrist. From that day, this despicable ex-captain had earned a livelihood as a wrecker, but he had never forgotten the grudge he owed to the Lord of Dunraven to whom he attributed his ruin . . .

'Some time later, one hot summer afternoon, while

Vaughan watched seaward, unknown to him, two of his younger sons set out in their father's boat for the Tuskar Rock, some mile and a half distant from the mainland; reaching there they moored the craft and gave themselves over to the pleasure of a swim.'

From his vantage point in a cave mouth 'Vaughan noticed that a wind was rising and clouds gathering; the sun, too, was sinking in a stormy setting. Suddenly, the ill-omened form of Matt-of-the-Iron-Hand was seen approaching; he advanced slowly, stopping every so often to shade his eyes as he looked intently out to sea toward Tuskar.

'Vaughan watched the man carefully, then the scoundrel's face was seen to change, a gleam of exultation came into his eyes and he uttered a sharp cry. Only then did Vaughan see his boat drifting off into the stormy sea, and the awful truth flashed into his mind. His two sons were stranded on the Tuskar and no boat could reach them in time. Distracted, he rushed down to the foreshore and from the Rock his sons could see him as he frantically waved to them. They were beyond his help. The seas rose higher until the two boys were overwhelmed and died before their father's eyes . . .

'The events of the day were considered . . . a just retribution on a man who had gotten his gains by luring seamen to their destruction by false beacons . . .'

Thus chastened, Vaughan's only preoccupation now was to scan the horizon out to sea for the ship that would bring his son home. One wild evening, such a ship approached the Welsh headlands.

'Vaughan was conscious of a strange anxiety about the ship, an anxiety he could not understand; moreover, he was fearful of Matt-of-the-Iron-Hand, whose vindictive hate was now unmistakable. The night darkened and grew thick; the wind rose and drizzling rain set in. Vaughan had not been long in his cave before the false lights of the ex-pirate threw a lurid light across the breakers. Listening intently, Vaughan heard, above the howling wind, the crashing sound of a ship being thrown on the rocks, wild and broken cries for help; then all was still and silent. In some thirty minutes the wrecker entered the cave where Vaughan still waited and told him that the ship's crew had taken to the boats as soon as their vessel struck and that they had then been swamped by seas and drowned; all but one member of the crew had died. The sole survivor, Matt-of-the-Iron-Hand said, turned out to be the captain, who had said that he was a Welshman and a native of Dunraven.

' "Were you able to save him?" asked Vaughan.

'A devilish laugh was the answer as the wrecker thrust a death-cold hand into that of Vaughan. A gleam of light from a fire in the cave lit up a ring on the dead hand . . . the ring Vaughan had given [his son] on the day [he] sailed away seeking his fortune.

'Matt-of-the-Iron-Hand had had his revenge in utter and final completion; recognising the captain of the ship as Vaughan's only remaining son, even though the sea had spared him, the wrecker had coldly slain him, and cutting off the hand with the distinctive family ring, had brought it to the stricken father.'

The demented man who runs along this part of the Glamorgan coast is thought by many to be Vaughan himself, while the wraith of the girl in white may be Vaughan's wife who shared so much tragedy with him.

The Haunted Isle of Scarba

Among the many Smaller Sudereys (the Inner, or Southern Hebrides) the island of Scarba, perhaps, can outmatch the coast of Glamorgan for its clamorous walking-dead. Resembling a dolphin in shape, Scarba is lofty with awe-inspiring cliffs and ranks among the most haunted islands in the world. Nearby is the great whirlpool of Corryvreckan, once reputed to be the lair of an enormous sea-beast and the headquarters of the powerful Celtic sea-gods.

Few fishermen if any, even today, will venture near Scarba's shore after dusk, for many a rumour tells of the dreadful cries echoing across the sea from Scarba, and of the strange eerie forms seen flitting along the shore in the light of the moon. But here are more sinister phantoms than ordinary ghosts and spectres.

Legend states that sailors who have been the most evil in mortal life come here as a penance after death and have to walk Scarba's cliffs for ever; some to be chased by the ghost of the famous Grey Dog, drowned between Scarba and Lunga, which belonged to Prince Breacan of Lochlarn (immortalised by Sir Walter Scott in *The Lord of the Isles*, 1815). As they run from the dog's fangs the phantom sailors must recite their crimes in a loud voice.

The Somerset Sea Morgan

Miss Ruth Tongue, the English folklorist, mentions in her *Somerset Folklore* (Folklore Society, London, 1965) hearing on September 29 1963 of 'the sea morgan and the conger eels', a story of how people could be lured into quicksands by mermaids[2]; sea morgan being the name for mermaid around the Severn Sea. Miss Tongue had first heard of this Somerset sea phantom from an old man in Taunton Red Cross Disabled Club. She later obtained a fuller account from a Stotford woman at the Eddington Women's Institute:

'There was a sea morgan with a beautiful face, and she'd sing on autumn evenings and anyone who heard her had to go, and they'd wade out further and further to reach her till the quicksands got them, and the conger eels got a feast.

---

[2]The dangerous and alluring qualities of mermaids—known since classical times—are exemplified in, Child, Francis J. *The English and Scottish Popular Ballads* (5 vols Dover Publications, New York, 1957) No 42 'Clerk Colvil'; and Chambers, Robert. *The Popular Rhymes of Scotland* (Edinburgh 1826) pp 279-80.

They always knew when the eels barked she would be about that low tide, so something was done to end her wicked ways.

'There was a gifted [ie psychic, or occultist] woman had a deaf son, and he was born on Sunday [once thought to be a protection against evil], so she sent him to drive away the morgan. He couldn't hear her voice, and as her hair was green, he didn't think much of her. He got out his Steart Horse [mud-sledge], and went out over the flats with his eel-spear, and all the while she was singing, he was getting a fine haul of congers, and the sled kept him from sinking in the quicksands. When he'd speared twelve of them, she gave a shriek, and took off—and she never come back.'

The Omen Tongues of Bells

Ghostly 'voices' of a different kind are also well repre-sented in the occultism of sea phantoms, these are called the 'omen tongues of bells'. The sound of church bells was once widely believed to drive away the sea demons which brought tempests and storm havoc, and the phantoms which constantly flitted about the shore seeking to harm the souls and bodies of fishermen and sailors. But seamen believe that a bell ringing on its own is an omen of disaster. This is reflected in the common coastal settlement superstition about the ringing note sometimes emitted by a tumbler or a wine glass, which foretells of a wreck at sea, or the death of a sailor (cf page 159).

During the days of sail, the ship's bell was regarded as in some sense embodying, along with the figurehead, a part of the ship's soul. Thus, sailors believed that it always 'spoke' when a wrecked ship went down, even if it had been securely lashed in place beforehand. Sometimes the final disaster did not always silence the bell.

In *Cornish Feasts and Folk-Lore* (1890), M. A. Courtney, for instance, tells of a ghostly bell which was often heard to strike four and eight bells in a churchyard near Land's End.

The sound, she wrote, came from the grave of a sea-captain who had refused to leave his sinking ship, when it was wrecked off the Cornish coast.

Apparently the captain went down in the ship exactly on midnight, as he was striking that hour on the bell. To hear this bell in the churchyard was indeed ominous, for Miss Courtney recorded how one sailor, out of bravado, once went to the grave to test the legend. He heard the bell toll, and was lost at sea on his next voyage!

The belief in drowned villages whose church bells sound from the deep as a storm warning, is a very widespread superstition in Britain, especially along the west coast.

The village of Kilgrimod, near Blackpool, Lancashire, for instance, was one such village drowned by the sea. Sailors who hear the phantom sexton tolling the bell of Kilgrimod church should never go to sea until 48 hours have elapsed. But it is lucky to hear Kilgrimod bells on Christmas Eve. Crowds of people used to go to this part of the beach along the coast of Lancashire on Christmas Eve in the hope of hearing the bells; to help themselves hear the bells they would lie full length on the sand or pebbles with ears pressed to the ground.

Once many centuries ago, tradition says, the sea in Nigg Bay, Ross and Cromarty, Scotland, was a low-lying and fertile valley. But a great storm arose and swept the sea between the fine pair of cliff headlands known as the Cromarty Suitors. All the fields and scrubland were thus submerged and buried in the sand, while a small village and its church were also covered by the sea.

Thereafter, sailors out of Cromarty and Moray Firth would 'listen' before setting sail. For danger was clearly forecast if they could hear the submerged churchbells of Nigg. Some of the old sailors hereabouts still tell of how the remnants of buildings of the submerged village could be clearly seen in the sea up to the late 1890s, but the last recorded phantom tolling was heard in the early 1920s.

Chapter 9

Dead Sailors Walk the Shore

The Phantom Prowler of Canvey Point

At Leighbeck the road from Hadleigh, Essex, vanishes and presently the traveller is among the wild fowl and decaying timbers of the old hulks which litter the mudflats thereabouts. For this is Canvey Point, where the seawall impedes the oily waters of the Thames Estuary, and where the bright lights of Southend flicker in the distance.

The lights, however, do not perturb the ghost which walks these shores at night, nor do the throbbing freighters and ocean-going liners disturb his patrol as they float down the river sending a wash of thick slime against the seawall. One of the many reported walking dead, who were sailors in mortal life, this ghost is 6 feet tall, fierce looking, with a beard and long moustaches. Wildfowlers and fishermen who have seen him say that he wears a horned helmet and jerkin of coarse leather. As the phantom strides out over the mud-flats, his long sword, hanging loose from his belt, sends a clanking sound through the ever-rustling reeds. All agree that the ghost is of a Viking, supposedly one of the horde of Danes who pillaged the Essex coast a thousand years ago.

The Limping Sailor of Chatham

The ghost of the limping sailor at St Mary's Naval Barracks, Chatham, however, is not as fierce as the Viking. In the log book at Chatham Naval Barracks this simple entry can be read: 'Ghost reported seen during middle watch'. This refers to the ghost of a peg-legged sailor of Admiral Lord Nelson's time. This ghost hobbles around with a

99

crutch and has been seen twice, in 1947 and 1949 in Room 34 of the Cumberland block, the oldest part of St Mary's Barracks. This apparition is thought to be the ghost of a sentry murdered by escaping French prisoners during the Napoleonic wars. The unfortunate sentry was apparently beaten to death as he was making for Room 34 to wake his relief, who was late for duty.

Quite often, so the old sailors say, those who have committed murder are doomed to sail the seas in the 'Devil's Phantom Bark'. This was the supposed fate of the drunken monks in the story of 'The Beauty of the Broads'.

The Beautiful Woman of Horning

Those who delight in boats know Horning, on the winding River Bure, one of the most popular yachting centres on the Norfolk Broads. In the height of summer the river is alive with craft which assemble and remain for September's week-long regatta. Every 20 years, crowds gather in the hope of seeing the ghost of a beautiful woman and the phantom ship which takes her brutal murderers on that everlasting voyage of penance.

About a mile or so downstream from Horning is the 'Old Ferry Inn', which centuries past was a meadhouse used by local monks who stocked the cellars with the homemade brew which was to see them through the harsh East Anglian winter. Here, late one summer's day, a local beauty was waylaid by drunken monks who raped her and flung the ravaged corpse into the river.

On the reappearance of the girl's ghost on September 25 1936, the inn's then licensee reported: 'I was awaiting the return of a resident. It was about midnight. I was dozing. Then suddenly I was wide awake. I heard a noise, a rustling. Not three yards away from me, in the passage leading to the staircase, was the frail shadowy form of a girl of about twenty-five. She wore a greenish grey cloak, but it was her face that most attracted my attention. It was beautiful yet deathly white and had a look of suffering.

'I spoke to her and went towards her, but she glided in front of me towards the door. She appeared to go through the door. I opened it and followed and was just in time to see her disappear at the edge of the river near the chain ferry.'

Another resident was able to corroborate the licensee's story. This witness had been sitting outside the front of the inn in the night air, smoking a last cigarette before retiring to bed: 'I heard the landlord cry out. The next moment the slim figure of this girl glided past me into the water; but I did not see her face.'

No doubt the river around the 'Old Ferry Inn' will be crowded in 1976, when the girl, and maybe her monastic murderers, are next due to reappear!

The Sailor Monks of Beaulieu Abbey

Perhaps because of their cloistered existence and their nearness to, and contemplation of, a spiritual world, monks seem to have a penchant for becoming ghosts after death. The ghostly sailor monks of Beaulieu Abbey, however, are not as bloodthirsty as those of East Anglia. Beaulieu Abbey, Hampshire, was founded in the year 1204 by the detested King John, who, according to legend, was moved to expiate his hatred and persecution of the Cistercian monastic order. Today little is left of this great abbey which sheltered Margaret of Anjou after the battle of Barnet (1471). Between 1542 and 1544 King Henry VIII (1491-1547) used much of the abbey's stone for his nearby fortress of Hurst Castle. The Early English refectory is now, however, the parish church, and the former Great Gatehouse now forms part of the present Palace House, ancestral home of Lord Montagu of Beaulieu. People living in the neighbourhood still speak of the mystic influence the monks who once inhabited Beaulieu have.

One afternoon in July 1957, three local boys Colin Hillman, Roy Jenvey and Ben Ham were out fishing in a dinghy in the Solent. As the boys made for home the strong cross-currents carried them off course. By this time it had started to rain heavily and the boys decided to make for the nearest point on the shore in order to shelter. Eventually they beached the boat and found shelter in a disused boat-house. Close on midnight the weather had worsened. An hour later the boys had become restless and Roy Jenvey opened the boathouse door to see if there was any improvement in the weather. As he watched the rain slanting across the beach, he caught sight of a rowing boat making for the shore.

The three boys watched as five hooded men stepped out of the boat. The men, dressed in the white habit of monks, filed away up the beach in the direction of Beaulieu Abbey. At dawn when it had faired the boys examined the shore where they had seen the monks land; there was no trace of a boat, nor of any footprints in the sand. Later, as the story was retold to parents and friends, no-one could offer a logical explanation for what the boys had seen.

The Ballyheigue Castle Mystery

Ballyheigue (pronounced 'balleyhigh') is a small fishing village with a majestic castle on the Atlantic coast of Eire. Once swarming with smugglers, this part of the Irish coast is quieter now, although a favourite spot with tourists.

In June 1962, Captain P. D. O'Donnell and his family were holidaying at Ballyheigue and encountered by chance a strange phantom sailor. Captain O'Donnell later recorded his experiences of the ghost in the magazine *Ireland of the Welcomes* published by Bord Failte Eireann (the Irish Tourist Board).

One afternoon during this holiday O'Donnell and his eight-year-old son Frank set out to explore the shell of

Ballyheigue Castle. Once the stronghold of the Crosbie family, who had lorded it over County Kerry for many years, the castle had been burnt to the ground during the Irish 'troubles' of 1921. After some investigations of the ruins O'Donnell took several photographs of the mouldering walls and went home.

Curiously enough, when the photographs were developed, one was found to contain 'another figure' partly obscured by a square of light which had come from one of the castle windows. The figure held a sword and appeared to be clad in hose or thigh boots. Following careful examination of the proofs and negatives, O'Donnell and several of his friends agreed that the mysterious photograph was not the result of double exposure. Unfortunately, the only print of the snapshot and the negative were subsequently lost in transit to a friend. Try as he might, Captain O'Donnell was not able to find the missing picture, even though he advertised in the Irish newspapers and even had leaflets printed offering a substantial reward. In time, however, the news of his loss and reward travelled widely and O'Donnell had enquiries from as far away as Copenhagen offering to buy the Danish rights to the photograph.

Why were the Danes of all people so interested in the photograph of a ghost? Captain O'Donnell decided to investigate.

According to the old chronicles of Kerry, a Danish ship, the *Golden Lyon*, in the fleet of the Danish Asiatic Company *en route* from Copenhagen to Tranquebar, was wrecked off Ballyheigue strand on October 20 1730. Blown off course by a fierce storm, the *Golden Lyon* became easy prey for the ship-wrecking Crosbies, or so the old legends say. Some still tell how the Crosbies set up false lights on the heads of horses to lure ships ashore. Thinking that the bobbing lights ahead were from other shipping the helmsmen would steer towards them only to wreck their ships among the Atlantic breakers.

The crew of the *Golden Lyon* were 'rescued' by Sir Thomas

Crosbie and his men, who salvaged much of the Danish ship's cargo and some 12 chests of silver bars and coin.

Soon after, Sir Thomas Crosbie died suddenly (some say poisoned by his wife). His wife, Lady Margaret, immediately claimed £4,500.00 ($10,800.00) from the Danish ship's master Captain J. Heitman, for salvage and the loss of her husband, who she claimed had died 'of his labours and exertions on the night of the wreck'. Fearing for his 12 chests of silver Captain Heitman removed them into the castle's cellar for safe keeping, mounting a guard at the cellar door until he was able to ship the bullion back to Denmark.

One night shortly afterwards, the castle was raided and the chests of silver were stolen. The authorities subsequently only managed to recover some £5,000.00 ($12,000.00) out of the total £20,000.00 ($48,000.00) worth of silver. Lady Margaret was strongly implicated as having been an instigator of the raid, but publicly denied all knowledge of it. Today various local legends abound as to where the silver went.

Records state that the Danish Silver Raid took place on June 4 1731. Captain O'Donnell's photograph of the phantom sailor was taken on June 4 1962. Does the sailor, therefore, appear on the anniversary of the raid?

Certainly the silver (the £15,000.00 or so unaccounted for) may still lie somewhere underneath the crumbled walls of Ballyheigue Castle. As there are many other examples of ghostly spirits guarding treasure, maybe the phantom sailor of Ballyheigue Castle stands where the silver is hidden.

The Welsh Sea Captain

A Welsh ghost carries on a similar vigil. In 1955 Jack Rees was a 26-year-old steel erector employed at Carmarthen Bay Power Station. At the time of his brush with this phantom he was living at a house in Bryn Terrace, Llanelly with his

23-year-old wife and son of seven. For three years the Rees family had lived in this Llanelly house, but for some time before the climax of events they had been perturbed by 'knockings at the door with no one there, and smashed crockery galore'.

This down-to-earth family, however, little suspected that their lives were being affected by the occult, the first manifestations of which had been poltergeist activity—poltergeist being a compound of the German verb *poltern*, to rattle, and *Geist*, a ghost.

At midnight on June 2 1955, Jack Rees was awakened by what he took to be the sound of dripping water and made to get out of bed to investigate. In moving to pull off the bedclothes, however, he saw to his horror, an apparition some three feet from the bed. 'I stared at it', he later reported to the *Western Mail and South Wales News*, 'and studied it for some three minutes . . . It did not move. I jerked my head suddenly and it backed away. My wife woke up, took one look at it and screamed. It then disappeared'.

Once before, the Reeses had seen the apparition, this time on the landing. The bedside visitation, however, was quite enough for the Reeses—they moved!

Investigations in the neighbourhood of Bryn Terrace uncovered the theory that the apparition was the 'malevolent spirit' of an old retired sea captain. The captain had been a well-known miser when he had lived in the house around 1886. It was thought that this phantom returned from time to time to seek the money the captain had once mislaid in the house.

The Phantom Intruder

Mr and Mrs P. from the north of England had a similar visitation from a ghostly sailor. Mrs P. and her husband had just gone to bed, but Mrs P. was still in her dressing gown, prior to attending to her baby lying in the cot beside her.

A lamp was alight in the bedroom and the door was locked.

Mrs P. remembers: 'I was just pulling myself into a half-sitting position against the pillows, thinking of nothing but the arrangements for the following day, when I saw a man standing at the side of the bed dressed as a naval officer. He was leaning on his arms and hands, which rested on the bed.

'Touching my husband's shoulder—his face was turned away from me—I said, "Willie, who is this?"

'My husband turned his head for a second or two and looked in astonishment at the intruder. Then he shouted: "What on earth are you doing here, sir?"

'The form slowly drew itself into an upright position and said in a commanding, yet reproachful voice: "Willie, Willie".

'My husband's face was white and agitated. He sprang out of bed as though to attack the man, but stood by the bed as if afraid, while the figure calmly and slowly moved towards the wall.

'As it passed the lamp, a deep shadow fell on the room. He disappeared into the wall. The apparition had gone—and the door was still locked!'

Having searched the house and found nothing Mrs. P realised who the ghost had been: 'It was my father. He was a naval officer in his youth.' Her father had been dead for fourteen years at the time of the visitation!

Smuggler's Leap

The Isle of Thanet is a large promontory on the north-east extremity of Kent, formed by a bifurcation of the River Stour. Thanet contains Margate, Ramsgate and Broadstairs along with other popular seaside resorts. In Thanet, near what used to be called the 'Hamlet of Acol,' was a very deep but long-disused chalk-pit.

A traditional Thanet story[1] tells how an exciseman called Anthony Gill and a smuggler he was chasing, lost their lives in the chalk-pit sometime in the early 1700s. Thereafter known as 'Smuggler's Leap' many reported that they had seen the ghosts of the exciseman and smuggler struggling on the edge of the chalk-pit. So many sightings were reported that a poem was written to commemorate the tradition:

'The fire-flash shines from Reculver cliff,
And the answering light burns blue in the skiff,
And there they stand, that smuggling band,
Some in the water and some on the sand,
Ready those contraband goods to land:
The night is dark, they are silent and still,
At the head of the party is Smuggler Bill!

'Now lower away! come, lower away!
We must be far ere the dawn of the day.
If Exciseman Gill should get scent of the prey,
And should come, and should catch us here, what would he say?
Come, lower away, lads—once on the hill,
We'll laugh, ho! ho! at Exciseman Gill!'

'The cargo's lower'd from the dark skiff's side,
And the tow-line drags the tubs through the tide,
No trick nor flam, But your real Schiedam.
"Now mount, my merry men, mount and ride!"
Three on the crupper and one before,
And the led-horse laden with five tubs more;
But the rich point-lace, In the oil-skin case
Of proof to guard its contents from ill,
The "prime of the swag", is with Smuggler Bill!

---

[1]See: Pegg, Rev Samuel. *Supplement to Lewis's History of Thanet.* (W. Bristow. Canterbury 1796) 127.

'Merrily now in a goodly row,
Away and away those smugglers go,
And they laugh at Exciseman Gill, ho! ho!
When out from the turn   Of the road to Herne,
Comes Gill, wide awake to the whole concern!
Exciseman Gill, in all his pride,
With his Custom-house officers all at his side!
—They were called Custom-house officers then;
There were no such things as "Preventive men" . . .

'*Sauve qui peut*! That lawless crew,
Away, and away, and away they flew!
Some seek Whitstable—some Grove Ferry,
Spurring and whipping like madmen—very—
For the life! for the life! they ride! they ride!
And the Custom-house officers all divide,
And they gallop on after them far and wide!
All, all, save one—Exciseman Gill—
He sticks to the skirts of Smuggler Bill! . . .

'Smuggler Bill from his holster drew
A large horse-pistol, of which he had two!
Made by Nock; He pull'd back the cock
As far as he could to the back of the lock;
The trigger he touch'd, and the welkin rang
To the sound of the weapon, it made such a bang;
Smuggler Bill ne'er missed his aim,
The shot told true on the Dun[2]—but there came
From the hole where it entered—not blood—but flame;
He changed his plan, And fired at the man;
But his second horse-pistol flashed in the pan!
And Exciseman Gill, with a hearty good will,
Made a grab at the collar of Smuggier Bill.

'The dapple-grey mare made a desperate bound

---

[2]ie, Gill's horse.

Pride of the German Navy, the *Scharnhorst* was launched in 1936. Many said she was 'jinxed'; she was sunk by British action in 1943. (*Conway Picture Library.*)

The 22,500-ton *Great Eastern* was an unlucky ship for many of her captains and was thought to be haunted by a riveter's ghost. (*Author's Collections.*)

'Mummy cover from the coffin of an unknown princess from Thebes, XXI Dynasty.' This British Museum exhibit was nicknamed 'Ship Wrecker'. The superstitious believed the spirit of the dead princess caused disaster to the *Empress of Ireland,* the *Titanic* and *HMS Hampshire.* (*The British Museum.*)

The *Titanic* was launched at the Belfast shipyards of Harland and Wolff on May 31 1911. The last ship to use the distress call CQD ('come quick danger'), the *Titanic* with 1,316 passengers on board and a crew of 891, collided with an iceberg off Cape Race April 14-15 1912; over 1,500 lives were lost. (*The National Maritime Museum.*)

Sir Ernest Alfred Thompson Wallis Budge (1857-1934), for 30 years Keeper of the Egyptian and Assyrian Antiquities at the British Museum. This translator of the famous *Book of the Dead* believed in Ancient Egyptian magic, and the power of the dead princess. (*The British Museum.*)

HMS Hampshire in which Field Marshal Lord Kitchener died. Some still say that he was the victim of the Ancient Egyptian curse. (*The National Maritime Museum.*)

A modern Japanese photo-montage of the traditional sea spirit, which doubles in horror movies as the snake goddess (*Author's Collection.*)

Kongo-Rikishi or *Nio.* The name applied to two Japanese guardian gods, whose fierce looking statues are found standing on each side of the gate of a Buddhist temple. Particularly popular amongst Japanese sailors as protectors. (*Author's Collection.*)

When that queer Dun horse on her flank she found,
Alack! and alas! on what dangerous ground!
It's enough to make one's flesh to creep
To stand on that fearful verge, and peep
Down the rugged sides so dreadfully steep,
Where the chalk-hole yawns full sixty feet deep,
O'er which that steed took that desperate leap!
It was so dark then under the trees,
No horse in the world could tell chalk from cheese—
Down they went—o'er that terrible fall,—
Horses, Exciseman, Smuggler, and all!!

'Below were found Next day on the ground
By an elderly gentleman walking his round,
(I wouldn't have seen such a sight for a pound,)
All smash'd and dash'd, three mangled corpses,
Two of them human,—the third was a horse's—
That good dapple-grey, and Exciseman Gill
Yet grasping the collar of Smuggler Bill!

'But where was the Dun? that terrible Dun?
From that terrible night he was seen by none! . . .
You may hear old folks talk   Of that quarry of chalk . . .
. . . that fearful chalk-pit —so awfully deep,
Which is called to this moment "The Smuggler's Leap"
Nay more, I am told, on a moonshiny night,
If you're "plucky" and not over subject to fright,
And go and look over that chalk-pit white,
You may see . . . The Ghost of Old Gill
Grappling the Ghost of Smuggler Bill,
And the Ghost of the dapple-grey lying between 'em . . .'[3]

For superstitious folk the approach of death has always
been surrounded by signs, omens and portents. Whether the

---

[3]Ingoldsby, Thomas. *The Ingoldsby Legends, or Mirth and Marvels*. Series
1-3. (Richard Bentley, London, 1866) pp 288-93.

wheeling of a lone seagull above the masthead, or a sudden calm, anything unexplained serves the sailor as a warning of evil, or at the very least, death.

Apparitions of dying sailors have often been seen by people at a distance, either at the actual moment of death or just before it. Some scholars believe that such visions are not true hauntings but are caused by telepathy, or some kind of thought-transference from the mind of the dying person to the seer or psychic medium. This is a likely explanation in cases where the ghost appears to near relatives, or close friends, especially if they already know that death is immediately expected. Nevertheless there are cases of such visions when death was not expected; the Tryon case being a classic example.

At the Moment of Death

On the afternoon of June 22 1893, Lady Tryon gave an 'at home' in her house in Eaton Square, London. Sometime during the afternoon, several of Lady Tryon's guests saw the figure of a man they took to be her husband, Admiral Sir George Tryon, walk through the drawing-room. The man did not speak to anyone, and the guests were puzzled, for at the time Sir George was supposed to be in command of the Mediterranean Squadron, then on manoeuvres off the coast of Syria. At that moment, however, when the wraith of the admiral crossed the drawing-room he was in fact already dead.

To naval historians the events preceding Sir George's death are more extraordinary than the vision of his ghost seen by his wife's guests. At the exact time of the 'at home', Sir George's squadron was steaming in two columns; his flagship HMS *Victoria* leading one column, and the HMS *Camperdown*, commanded by Admiral Markham, leading the other.

During the manoeuvre Admiral Tryon signalled for the

two lines of ships to move closer. His exact instruction meant, of course, that the ships were in grave danger of collision. Only when it was too late did he order the ships to steam astern. Consequently the *Camperdown* crashed into the *Victoria* with a great loss of life[4]; Sir George was also killed.

No-one at the time, or at the subsequent enquiry could give a logical explanation why a competent, level-headed sailor had given such a disastrous order. As his ship was sinking, however, Sir George was heard to say: 'It is all my fault'.

To those who believe in ghost phenomena only one explanation seems to fit. As he realised in those last few awful moments what he had done, Sir George's agonised thoughts turned to his home in Eaton Square with such a force as to project his appearance in the drawing-room, where his wife, unconscious of the tragedy, was entertaining her friends[5].

Closely akin to the phantoms of the dying are those vivid dreams by which some sailors have been warned at sea of the death of others. On February 8 1840 one Nevell Norway was murdered by William and James Lightfoot. His brother Edmund Norway, then captain of the *Orient*, a merchant ship sailing from Manilla to Cadiz, recorded a vivid dream of his brother's death:

'Ship Orient, from Manilla to Cadiz
February 8, 1840

About 7.30 p.m., the island of St. Helena N.N.W. distant about 7 miles; shortened sail and rounded to with the ship's head to the eastward; at 8 set the watch and went below; wrote a letter to my brother Nevell Norway. About twenty

---

[4]Among the survivors was a young sailor who was later to be Commander-in-Chief of the British Fleet, Earl Jellicoe (1859-1935).

[5]For a further example of this type of sea phantom see page 122 seqq. of this book.

minutes or a quarter before ten o'clock, went to bed; fell asleep and dreamt I saw two men attacking my brother and murder him. One caught the horse by the bridle and snapped a pistol twice but I heard no report; he then struck him a blow and he fell off his horse. They struck him several blows and dragged him by the shoulders across the ground and left him. In my dream there was a house on the left-hand side of the road. At four o'clock I was called and went on deck to take charge of the ship. I told the second officer, Mr. Henry Wren, that I had had a dreadful dream—namely, that my brother Nevell was murdered on the road from St. Colomb to Wadebridge but I felt sure it could not be there, as the house there would have been on the right-hand side of the road; so that it must have been somewhere else. He replied: "Don't think anything about it; you west-country people are so superstitious. You will make yourself miserable the remainder of the voyage . . ." '

Strangely enough the road which Captain Norway remembered in his dream *had been altered* so that the house was now in reality on the left-hand side! The captain's dream proved thus to be an almost eye-witness account of the dreadful events which had taken place on the road between Bodmin and Wadebridge[6].

The Grey Lady of Great Isaac

No islands in the whole of the Atlantic can boast such a distinguished roster of tourists as the wonderful archipelago that extends some 800 miles from Florida south-east to the Dominican Republic. Many people think of the Bahamas as just Nassau. In fact there are about 700 islands and nearly 2,000 keys and rocks in the island chain, scattered like coral in the turquoise waters, extending across an area of 70,000 square miles.

---

[6]For further notes and commentary see: Baring-Gould, Sabine. *Cornish Characters and Strange Events* (London, 1925).

According to superstitions thereabouts, the main islands all have their ghosts and ghostships which usually date from the days of the pirates, privateers and buccaneers. The occult cult of the sea, however, has not entirely forsaken the sparsely inhabited resorts on the fringes of the Bahaman group—known as Out Islands. Today one such group, called the 'magical' Biminis by the inhabitants, not only boasts the best game fishing in the world, but also the most famous seashore phantom in the area, known as 'The Grey Lady of Great Isaac'.

Great Isaac Lighthouse is located some 35 miles from Gun Cay on the Bimini group. The only tower in the Bahama lighthouse system to be constructed of cast-iron, the imposing structure stands some 152 feet above sea level and directs a powerful beam of 500,000 candlepower out across the Strait of Florida. The lighthouse was completed on August 1 1859 and, because it was the first to be erected in the Bahamas after the accession of Queen Victoria, it was popularly known as the 'Victoria Light'[7].

This legend of the walking dead comes from the private and authenticated notes of Commander R. Langton-Jones, a former inspector of the Bahamas Imperial Lighthouse Service.

'Some two years before the tower was erected, a terrific hurricane blew in from the south and passed right over the Cay, leaving in its wake a long trail of death and destruction. Innumerable ships were trapped in its path and sunk or driven ashore . . . [thereafter] . . . above the moaning of the wind [fishermen] were suddenly startled to hear a series of uncanny cries.

'Eyes straining shoreward, they were astonished to see a strange sight, in the shape of a white horse stumbling heavily among the jagged rocks. With much trepidation and

---

[7]See: *Illustrated London News*, issue of 24.9.1859, for full pictorial details of the building operations.

fear the men shortened sail, swung their vessel inshore, and there decided to land and investigate further . . . and discovered the object of their search. Stretched on the barren ground lay a handsome white horse, its neck broken, dead. How had this animal reached the forbidding Cay? The men decided to search the foreshore and at a short distance from where the present lighthouse stands they were horrified to find the rocks strewn with mutilated bodies, some half-buried beneath the pathetic flotsam of a recent wreck, thrown up by the seas . . . among the corpses, already stiffened in the cold embrace of death, was that of a young woman tightly clasping to her breast the body of a child . . . [A] miracle had happened . . . the baby was still breathing [and] had suffered no bodily hurt . . . it was subsequently adopted by a couple living in Bimini. The child was afterward taken to England . . .'[8]

One night, during the month of November in the year 1858, a member of the working party engaged in the erection of the tower breathlessly entered the bunkhouse where his comrades were congregated and excitedly told them that he had seen, in the light of the rising moon, the figure of a woman in white making her way slowly among the rocks skirting the foreshore, stopping at frequent intervals as if searching for something she had lost. Upon his approach she disappeared.

At first his story was laughed off as a joke, but very soon afterwards the foreman of the erection crew, who had walked to the sea's edge to watch a passing ship, was terror-stricken to behold suddenly the same uncanny and mysterious figure.

On various dates between the years 1858 and 1913 this supernatural occurrence was reported by a succession of

---

[8] Taken from discovered notes of R. Langton-Jones. See: Catalogue Biblioteca Central—Rubén Martinez Villena—de la Universidad de la Habana.

lighthouse keepers. On repeated occasions the wraith was observed from the foreshore, and, at times, seen to hover momentarily in the shadow of nearby dwellings . . . [it appeared] eternally searching . . . In 1913, the chief keeper at Great Isaac was coming off watch shortly after ten o'clock one night, and as he slowly descended the spiral stairway of the tower he observed the white phantom moving towards him slowly, upward. Her hooded head was bent forward . . . Steadily the white figure advanced in his direction, but just as he recovered his senses sufficiently to turn and run, the white figure moved away and then vanished . . .

In 1914, when the first routine change of keepers took place at Great Isaac, the chief keeper, anxious not to encounter the ghost himself, attempted to exorcise the spirit. At dusk, on that part of the Cay where the drowned had been washed ashore, he held a solemn committal service for the dead. After that the 'Grey Lady of Great Isaac' was seen no more.

The Ghostly Victorian Seafarer

The 'Shipwright's Arms' is a thirteenth-century part-weatherboarded inn overlooking the melancholy marshlands of Hollow Shore, between Oare and Faversham, Kent. Should the visitor to this inn be told that the house was *not* haunted, they would undoubtedly be disappointed. For in the whole of the British Isles, this hostelry has all the ingredients of a haunted inn. On a thick winter's night, when the distant fog-horns blow, few would wander out hereabouts, especially those who had heard the story of the ghostly Victorian seafaring man with the glaring eyes and the dark reefer jacket.

Whenever this ghost appears, a strong unfamiliar smell accompanies him. The wife of one of the inn's licensees once said: 'I saw the [ghost] standing at the bottom of the bed, just looking at me . . . I experienced the same thing on three consecutive nights, and I have also seen the man sitting in the small room adjoining the bar . . .'

A boatbuilder from the shipyard next to the inn also saw the seaman's ghost. One night the boatbuilder was alone in the bar when he felt a cold draught at his back, and heard the door close. A bearded sailor in a long black coat came into the bar and disappeared into thin air. On another occasion the boatbuilder was sleeping at the yard where he worked, when he was awakened by a ghostly hand! He saw nothing, only felt the grip of this, one of the many phantom sailors who regularly walk the shore!

Chapter 10

Leaves from a Ghosthunter's Notebook

Phantoms of St Ives Bay

F ishermen at St Ives, Cornwall, still remember the night when they were called upon to go to the rescue of a vessel which had been burning lights as a signal for help to the westward of St Ives Head.

When the rescuers drew near the stricken vessel, they saw to their astonishment that her masts and rigging were coated with ice, as if she had come through Arctic weather. No one was visible on deck, and no one replied when the ship was hailed. But stranger things were to follow.

As the man in the bows of the St Ives rescue boat tried to grab hold of the bulwarks of the strange vessel, the latter suddenly disappeared and the man would have fallen into the sea had he not been held by his mates.

Older fishermen among the rescuers recounted the story about the famous phantom ship of St Ives Bay, as the rescuers rowed home. The phantom ship is seldom seen off St Ives, except before some naval disaster. A few hours after the men returned, however, a terrific storm arose and a ship was wrecked at Gwithian, everyone aboard perishing.

Port Danger

During 1821 a small squadron of ships, including the brig *HMS Barracouta*, led by *HMS Severn*, were surveying the coasts of Arabia, Africa and Madagascar. In his log Captain

Owen, commanding *HMS Severn* reported that the squadron was dispersed off the Cape and then continued:

'In the evening of April 6th, when off Port Danger, the *Barracouta* was seen about two miles to leeward. Struck with the singularity of her being so soon after us, we at first concluded that it could not be she; but the peculiarity of her rigging and other circumstances convinced us that we were not mistaken. Nay, so distinctly was she seen that many well-known faces could be observed on deck, looking towards our ship.

'After keeping thus for some time, we became surprised that she made no effort to join us, but on the contrary stood away. But being so near to the port to which we were both destined . . . we did not attach much importance to this proceeding and . . . continued our course. At sunset it was observed that she hove to and sent a boat away, apparently for the purpose of picking up a man overboard. During the night we could not perceive any light or indication of her locality. The next morning we anchored in Simon's Bay, where for a whole week we were in anxious expectation of her arrival; but it afterwards appeared that at this very period the *Barracouta* must have been above three hundred miles from us, and no other vessel of the same class was ever seen about the Cape'.

So many sightings of sea phantoms had been received from ships in the Table Bay area of the Cape, that the British Commissioners of Admiralty did not think the Port Danger incident unusual. Captain Owen's signal was filed away among the many cases known as 'Flying Dutchman—Miscellaneous'.

The Ghost in York Cathedral

In the book *Accredited Ghost Stories*, collected by T. M. Jarvis (London, 1823) this curious tale appeared:

'It is not many years ago since Mr B---- L---- accompanied

some friends on a visit to York Cathedral:[1] the party was numerous, and amongst them were a gentleman and his two daughters. Mr B---- L---- was with the eldest of these ladies, exploring the curiosities of the building, rather at a distance from the rest of their companions. On turning from the monument to which their attention had been directed, an officer in a naval uniform was observed advancing towards them. It was rather an unusual circumstance to encounter a person thus accoutred in a place so far distant from the sea, and of so unmilitary a character. Mr B---- L---- was on the point of making a trivial observation on the subject to his companion, when, on turning his eyes towards her and pointing out the approaching stranger to her notice, he saw an immediate paleness spread over her face, and her countenance became agitated by the force of the powerful and contending emotions which were suddenly excited by his presence.

'As the stranger drew more near, and his figure and his features gradually became more distinctly visible through the evening gloom and the dim religious light of the cathedral, the lady's distress was evidently increased; she leant on the arm of Mr B---- L---- with the weight of one who was painfully afflicted and felt the necessity of support. Shocked at the oppression which he witnessed, but wholly ignorant of the cause—alarmed—hurried—supposing her to be suffering from the paroxysm of some violent and sudden indisposition, Mr B---- L---- called to entreat the assistance of her sister. The figure in the naval uniform was now immediately before them: the eyes of the lady were fixed upon him with a gaze of silent and motionless surprise and a painful intensity of feeling; her lips were colourless and apart, and her breath passed heavily from the full and overburthened heart.

'The form was close upon them:—it approached her side:

---

[1]York's great cathedral is invariably referred to as 'The Minster', or 'York Minster'.

—it paused but for an instant:—as quick as thought, a low and scarcely audible voice whispered in her ear—"There is a future state"; and the figure moved onward through the retiring aisle of the minster.

'The father of the lady arrived to the assistance of his daughter, and Mr B---- L---- consigning her to his protection. hastened in pursuit of the mysterious visitor. He searched on every side: no such form was to be seen in the long perspective of the path by which the illomened stranger had departed. He listened with the most earnest attentiveness: no sound of retreating footsteps was to be heard on the echoing pavement of the cathedral.

'Baffled in his attempt to discover the object whose presence had thus disturbed the tranquillity of the time, Mr B---- L---- resought his friends. The lady was weeping on the shoulder of her father; she avoided every enquiry respecting the cause, the seat, and the nature of her illness:—"It was slight; it was transient; it would immediately be over." She entreated the party to continue their examination of the building, and to leave her again in the protection of her former companion. The request was granted; and no sooner had she thus possessed herself of an opportunity of confidential communication than she implored him, with a quick and agitated voice, to conceal for a little while the occurrence of which he had been a witness:—

' "We shall never be believed: besides, it were right that my poor dear father should be gradually prepared for the misery that he is destined to undergo. I have seen the spirit, and I have heard the voice of a brother, who exists no longer: he has perished at sea. We had agreed that the one who died the first should reappear to the survivor, if it were possible, to clear up or to confirm the religious doubts which existed in both our minds."

'In due time the account of the event arrived to verify the spiritual intimation: the brother was indeed no more. His death had happened on the very day and hour in which his form was seen by Mr B---- L---- and his sister, in the north aisle of York Cathedral.'

A Uist Spectre Ship

Spectre ships have been long seen on the coast of Uist (Outer Hebrides, Inverness, Scotland)[2], and one particular story was often related by Shony Campbell (Seonaidh Caimbeul) the famous storyteller and Gaelic poet.

One New Year's Day, Shony Campbell and a companion were returning home from fishing. As they sailed home to Lochboisdale (the main harbour of South Uist), Campbell saw a splendidly rigged large ship coming northwards past Rubha na h-Òrdaig ('The Headland of the Thumb'—a promontory in South Uist, south of Bágh Hàrtabhagh Bay). The ship came close to the small boat and Campbell noticed that there was no name on her bows. After a while the ship turned out again to sea. Some two miles out at sea the ship was seen to belch smoke and all the while flounder deeper in the water. By this time Campbell realised that the ship was really sinking. Within minutes the white painted gunwaled ship had sunk and nothing more was seen of her.

On reaching land Campbell informed the Receiver of Wrecks of what they had seen. Curiously enough nothing was ever heard of the ship again, and no ship of similar description was ever reported missing.

Hoodoo aboard the Great Eastern

All the world watched in amazement as the great wonder grew at the Isle of Dogs on the Thames. Poets, engineers, commonfolk and kings all jostled to view the biggest vessel then afloat: The 692-foot long Great Eastern, mother of ocean liners.

---

[2]See: Campbell, J. L. and Hall, T. H. Strange Things. (Routledge & Kegan Paul, London, 1968). pp 272-74.

For more than a decade the shipping companies of America and Britain had glowered at each other across the Atlantic. Each battling with the other for mastery of the world's most lucrative trade route: the North Atlantic. Since the 1840s two shipping magnates, Sir Samuel Cunard (1785-1865) and the Massachusetts-born Edward Knight Collins (1802-78), had competed to build ships which could clip an extra hour or two off the New York-Liverpool and London-Boston crossings. Cunard's early 1,000-tonners and Collins's later 3,000-tonners were, however, to be dwarfed by this new giant, the *Great Eastern*, lauded in the headlines as 'The Wonder of the Seas'. Fully laden, the *Great Eastern* was to outweigh the combined tonnage of Britain's 197 ships which had fought the Spanish Armada. At full speed she was to outrace any vessel in the world. Searching for epithets the engineers aboard the *Great Eastern* were lost for words. The only size analogy to be found for the *Great Eastern* was in that of Noah's Ark: the Ark's gross tonnage[3] of 18,231 tons was to be greatly overshadowed by the *Great Eastern's* 22,500-ton displacement.

Under the watchful eye of her progenitor Isambard Kingdom Brunel (1806-59), successful builder of bridges and railroads, the monster ship took shape and 2,000 workers scuttled like insects among the prodigious parts of the ship. To one observer her screw was reminiscent of 'the blade bones of some huge animal of the pre-Adamite world', her hull plates would have 'formed shields for the gods', and her paddle wheels were 'larger than a one-ringed circus'.

To carry the 6,500 square yards of sail, the double-hull, the 112 furnaces, two 58-foot paddle-wheels, a 24-foot propeller the *Great Eastern* required 3,000,000 rivets, each one inch thick, and all hand-driven by two hundred rivet gangs.

Yet as the work went on apace, the hoodoo now asso-

---

[3]Originally worked out by Britain's greatest man of science Sir Isaac Newton (1642-1727).

ciated with the *Great Eastern*, which Brunel intended for the Australian run, began to take its toll. One worker fell to his death, another was crushed within the hull casing, and yet another fell on a workmate and killed him. A workboy[4] fell head first from the structure and was impaled on a jutting iron bar, and a casual visitor was mortally felled when a 'monkey came down, flattening his head'. One workman, 'a basher' (riveter), was reported missing while working amidships and was never seen again by his workmates.

On November 2 1857 the *Great Eastern* lay on the Thames water-front awaiting her launching at noon the next day. Because of her size she had been built broadside-on to the river. She was expected to slip quite easily into the Thames from this position, especially as she would be assisted by Brunel's specially constructed hydraulic rams.

A large crowd of Londoners braved the cold weather to watch the launching and all fell silent as an engineer waved his white flag to release the bow and stern fastenings, and to slacken off the chain provided to check the mighty ship's rate of slide. For a while nothing happened, and then the huge ship gave a shuddering rumble and creaked for a full ten minutes without moving. Eventually one man watching in the crowd yelled 'She moves! She moves!' and all saw the *Great Eastern's* stern begin to slide. The mud quaked beneath the mammoth hull and all who stood around felt the earth vibrate. The ship began to take up the slack chain and sent the windlass spinning in reverse, so that the huge handlebars struck a group of men and sent them hurtling above the heads of the crowd.

The *Great Eastern* shuddered with a terrible complaint of iron—men on the barge crews jumped into the river in panic (two were drowned)—and abruptly stopped. Again the hoodoo struck the *Great Eastern*; it was to be many months

---

[4]Children worked on the construction of the *Great Eastern* mostly as 'riveter's mates' or tenders of the rivet forges.

before she was to get afloat and many more to fit her out for ocean travel.

Isambard Kingdom Brunel was too ill to watch his monster ship go down the Thames to the sea on September 9 1859. But the day before Brunel's death (September 15 1859), Captain Harrison (later drowned) complained to his chief engineer that his rest had been 'rudely awakened by constant hammering from below'. No-one could account for the hammering and some muttered that the *Great Eastern* was haunted. Why else, they reasoned, had her progress been so blighted?

Four hours after she set off down the Thames one of the *Great Eastern's* five smoke stacks blew out killing six members of the engine-room crew and wrecking the grand saloon. Thus was the *Great Eastern's* career marred by storm and accident. Although the *Great Eastern* made several successful transatlantic crossings, in the end she became a costly 'white elephant of the seas', even serving as a vast showroom for the stocklines of Messrs Lewis' the famous English firm of clothiers and drapers. Strangely enough, each catastrophe in the *Great Eastern's* career was preceded by an unaccountable spate of hammering somewhere in the bowels of the ship!

Eventually, after much misfortune, the *Great Eastern* was stripped of her ornate and elegant furnishings and between 1865 and 1866 she helped lay a section of the first North Atlantic cable. The ship was sold for scrap in 1887.

As the tugboats drew the *Great Eastern* on her last journey to the breaker's yard, the mysterious hammering was heard again. This time the great ship slipped her lines and was nearly wrecked. Only by a superhuman effort was she brought to the breaker's yard of Henry Bath & Sons.

The breaking up of the *Great Eastern* began on January 1 1889. One day as a group of men were breaching the wall of a compartment in the *Great Eastern's* inner shell on the port side, they found a carpet bag of rusted tools, and alongside, a skeleton. Presumably these were the remains of the missing 'basher', who had accidentally been entombed between the hulls during some stage of the *Great Eastern's* construction[5].

For over 30 years, therefore, the superstitious said, the ghost of this unfortunate workman had hammered on the hull of the *Great Eastern* to warn of approaching misfortune.

Saga of the Scharnhorst

The German ship *Scharnhorst* was also thought to have a hoodoo.

Scharnhorst was a 32,000-ton naval weapon of supreme efficiency, but was a very unpopular vessel. Long before she was seaworthy *Scharnhorst* was declared jinxed by the men who worked on her hull, and, in spite of her speed, super-range guns and electronic equipment, no one wanted to serve aboard her.

She had been hardly half completed when the evil influences around *Scharnhorst* began to be manifest. Wrenching away from her supports, she rolled over on her side killing 61 workmen and injuring 110. Because of the jinx, work-gangs had to be regularly redrafted. Eventually she was dredged from where she had turned turtle and made ready for launching.

Scharnhorst was such a prize that the Nazi government eagerly made preparations to show her to the world. Particularly, Adolf Hitler wanted to impress the allied, neutral and enemy nations of Europe with the strength and supremacy of German arms. *Scharnhorst*, however, did not wait for the official launching. On the night previous to the official ceremony, where Hitler, Himmler, Goering and Goebbels were to stand smugly by the slipway, the mighty ship broke her cables and launched herself, smashing two barges in the process.

---

[5]See: Dugan, James. *The Great Iron Ship*. (Hamish Hamilton, 1953). pp 218-19.

Her first foray was in the seizure of Danzig. Later, the Nazi high command issued worldwide a news film of the *Scharnhorst's* mighty guns reducing the famous port (now called Gdansk) to rubble. What the film did not feature, however, was the nine men killed when one of the *Scharnhorst's* guns exploded, and the scene in another gun-turret where the air-conditioning failed and killed another 12 men.

In the Norwegian campaign *Scharnhorst* was badly crippled and was towed away by the *Gneisenau*. On her way home in the mouth of the Elbe the *Scharnhorst's* radar failed and the great ship collided with the liner *Bremen*.

It was to be a long time before *Scharnhorst* was back in action, this time attacking an Allied convoy in the Arctic Sea. Here along the coast of Norway she was outclassed by the British protective force. Under heavy fire *Scharnhorst* sank. Out of the *Scharnhorst's* 36 survivors two did not escape the evil influence of the sunken leviathan. Some months later the two men were found dead, killed by the explosion of an emergency oil stove.

Captain Alldridge's Tale

Captain George Manley Alldridge (1815-1905) was as old as his ship *HMS Asp*, a somewhat weather-beaten paddle-wheeler. *HMS Asp* had begun her life as the *Fury*, a vessel of 112 tons, with 120 horse-power engines and a length of 89 feet 7 inches. Used mostly as a mail packet ship, the *Fury* had regularly plied the Donaghadee (on the thin tongue of land in the Irish Sea which curves upwards towards Belfast Lough, County Down) to Portpatrick (on the west side of the hammerhead Rhinns of Galloway, Wigtownshire, Scotland) mail and passenger run.

In 1837, the Admiralty bought *Fury* from the British Post Office and refitted her as a survey ship, renaming her *HMS Asp*. What could not be changed, however, was the fact that the ship was haunted.

Looking for a 'good ghost story', a reporter from the *Pembroke County Gazette* contacted Captain Alldridge with the request for an interview about the haunted ship. Alldridge, being a man who hated publicity, refused the interview but wrote a letter giving full details of 'the unaccountable apparition'.

'March 15 1867. My dear Sir: . . . Many years have elapsed since I served in [*HMS Asp*] . . . In the year 1850 the *Asp* was given me by the Admiralty as a surveying vessel. On taking possession of her, the Superintendent of the Dockyard, where she lay, remarked to me: "Do you know, sir, your ship is said to be haunted? I doubt very much if you will get any of the Dockyard men to work on her much longer." . . . I said: "I don't care for ghosts, and I dare say I shall get her all to rights fast enough."

'I engaged the shipwrights to do the remaining necessary repairs and refit . . . the vessel, but before they had been working in her a week they came to me . . . and begged me to give the vessel up as she was haunted and could never bring anything but ill luck. However, she was at length repaired, and arrived safely in the River Dee, where she was to commence her duties. After my tea in the evening, I generally sat in my cabin and either read to myself or had an officer . . . read aloud to me . . . on such occasions we used frequently to be interrupted by strange noises, often such as would be caused by a drunken man, or a person staggering about, which appeared to issue from the after (or ladies', as it had been formerly, when the ship was on civilian service) cabin.

'The two cabins were only separated from each other by the companion ladder, the doors faced each other, so that from my cabin I could see into the after one. There was no communication between either of them and the other parts of the ship, excepting by the companion ladder which no one could ascend or descend without being seen from my own cabin. The evening shortly after our arrival in the

River Dee, the officer . . . was reading to me . . . when all at once his voice was drowned by a violent and prolonged noise in the after cabin. Thinking it must be my steward, he called out "Don't make such a noise, there", and thereupon the noise ceased. When he began to read again the noise also commenced.

' "What the hell are you doing, steward, making such a damned awful noise for?" he cried out, and taking a lamp off my table rushed into the next cabin. [The officer found nothing and returned]. He recommenced reading and once more the mysterious noise began. I felt sure there was some drunken person there whom the officer had not noticed and accordingly rose and looked for myself, and to my very great surprise found the cabin quite empty.'

After that the mysterious noises became more frequent, but no accountable reason for them could be found. Sometimes, while asleep in his cabin, Captain Alldridge was conscious 'of the presence of something invisible' near him, but never saw anything. Until:—

'One night, when the ship was at anchor in Martyn Roads, I was awakened by the quartermaster calling me . . . to come on deck as the lookout man had [seen] the figure of a woman . . . standing on the starboard paddle-box pointing with one finger to the skies.'

From then on the ghostly figure of the woman was seen more often, and strangely enough the sweet smell of perfume always followed her appearance.

Once the ghost actually spoke to a steward who promptly resigned the service! Over the years Captain Alldridge lost many of his crew, through desertion and resignation because of the ghost.

'At length, in 1857, the vessel requiring repairs was ordered alongside the dockyard wall at Pembroke. The first night the sentry stationed near the ship saw (as he later declared on oath) a woman mount the starboard paddle-box holding up her right hand to the skies.

'The phantom figure then stepped on shore and came along the path towards him, when he brought his musket to the charge and called: "Who goes there!" But the figure appeared to walk right through the musket, upon which the terrified man dropped it and fled for the guard-house. The next sentry saw all this take place and fired off his own gun to rouse the guard. The phantom figure then glided past a third sentry who was on duty near the ruins of Pater Old Church; the man watched her . . . mount the top of a grave in the churchyard, point with a finger to the skies, and then stand quite still until she vanished from sight . . .

'. . . since that particular . . . night, the ghost was not heard of again on board the *Asp* . . . Some years previous to my having her, the *Asp* had been engaged as a mail packet . . . After one of her trips, the passengers having all disembarked, a stewardess on going into the ladies' cabin discovered a very beautiful girl with her throat cut, lying in one of the sleeping berths . . . How she came by her death no one could tell . . . strict investigations were commenced . . . But . . . neither who she was nor where she came from, nor anything at all about her, has ever been discovered.'

From 1869 to 1880 *HMS Asp* was employed on work in connection with Chatham Dockyard extension. In 1881 the haunted ship was broken up.

Ghost Pictures in the Sea

In January 1925, an oil tanker was making her way through the Isthmus of Panama when two of the crew were overcome by fumes while washing down the empty cargo hatches. They both died of poisoned lungs the same night and were buried at sea.

A few days later, some of the crew were leaning over the rails on the port side, when in the water there appeared their two dead comrades. The men immediately reported the matter to the captain, who refused to believe the story, even though several of the ship's officers corroborated the facts. The men said that their dead mates' heads had appeared in the water for a few minutes at regular intervals and had then disappeared. The captain was still not convinced and at their next port of call he bought a camera in order to try and pin-point the evidence. Armed with this equipment, the captain waited with his men until the faces appeared as they approached the Isthmus and took six photographs.

The film was developed soon after, and five of the photographs showed nothing but waves and spray, but on the sixth was clearly seen what appeared to be the outlines of two heads and faces in the water. The photographs were later enlarged and examined by a specialist in psychic phenomena who, in doing an independent survey, showed that one of the faces in the photograph was definitely that of one of the dead men. The specialist could give no explanation.

The Phantom Landing Craft

It was reported in October 1959 that a 500-ton landing craft (said to be flying the flag of the Free French Forces of World War II) was in distress somewhere along the Devonshire coast. Two British warships and other vessels in the area raced to her aid. Soon the craft was sighted, but she appeared totally deserted and did not answer signals. When the British vessels *Acute*, *Turmoil* and *Torquay* sped to the craft's aid she disappeared into thin air—no one saw her again.

Drake's Drum

Among the few cases of sea phantom phenomena bringing omens of good fortune, is the curious case of 'Drake's Drum'. The drum, which the great admiral Sir Francis Drake (c 1540-96) is thought to have carried with him on his voyage round the world, is now held by Plymouth City Museum.

Tradition states that when the great man lay dying he asked that the drum be taken back to Devon, and promised that, if anyone beat upon the drum when England was in danger, he would return from the dead and lead her to victory. Devonshire superstition still has it that Drake did return twice, not, however, in his mortal form, but reincarnated as Admiral Robert Blake (1599-1657) and Horatio Nelson (1758-1805). Now it is said the drum sounds without the help of human hands to presage war. Its sound was clearly heard by many in November 1918.

On that misty day in the North Sea, the British Fleet was on patrol, led by *HMS Royal Oak* flying the silk banner made by Devon women. On the bridge of the *Royal Oak* Admiral Grant, Captain MacLachlan and other officers assembled. Around 9.00 am the German High Seas Fleet was sighted through the haze, and almost simultaneously a small drum began to beat 'rolls' somewhere aboard the *Royal Oak*. Puzzled by the sound, the senior officers sent messengers to every part of the ship to track down the drummer. No drummer was found and every man was marked present. Yet the drum continued to beat.

All the time the British Fleet was encircling the German ships the drum continued to beat. By 2.00 pm the enemy fleet had been completely surrounded and was helpless. As the British ships dropped anchor 15 miles off the Firth of Forth the drum fell silent. Over the ship's internal communication system came the simultaneous signal that the German Fleet had surrendered.

Folk around Combe Sydenham claimed to have heard 'Drake's Drum' as a prelude to World War II. *Drake's Drum*, a poem by John Henry Newbolt (1862-1938), commemorates the general belief.[6]

---

[6]See: *Collected Poems* 1897-1907 (London, 1910) 15-17.

Chapter 11

Occult Supplement
on the British Royal Navy

N o discussion of sea occultism would be complete without a postscript on some of the mystiques of the
British Royal Navy. Britain has had a navy of sorts since the
days of Caius Julius Caesar (c 101-44 BC), who wrote in his
De Bello Gallico how, when he attacked the Veneti of Gaul,
(merchant) ships from Britannia were there to help against
him. It is from these early times that the occultism of the
Royal Navy has its roots. Today in the Royal Navy, material-
ism and mechanics have robbed the sailor of his occult
traditions, but several of them still survive and have been
absorbed in part by other navies.

On page 185 of the following chapter, the custom of
Saluting the Quarter Deck is mentioned; another such
custom is Piping the Side, in which a high ranking officer is
'piped' aboard. In the days of the galley slaves of the Greek
and Roman ships, a pipe, or flute, was used as a timekeeper
for the stroke of the slaves at the oars. This is the most
probable origin of the boatswain's pipe of today. In the
chronicles of the Crusades it is recorded how English
crossbowmen were piped to action during sea-battles; In his
The Tempest William Shakespeare (1564-1616) mentioned
this boatswain's pipe.

In time the pipe became a badge of office, a mark of
honour and an occult symbol. While the Lord High Admiral
always carried a gold pipe on a chain round his neck as a
sign of his exalted rank, old instructions read how such
officers should blow 'three several times' for 'good luck' on
auspicious occasions.

Occult significance has always played a great part in launching ceremonies, for to sailors this was as important as the baptism of infants. Thus, both had to be protected from the 'evil eye' (see: *A Book of Superstitions* and *A Book of Witchcraft*). There again, the superstition of propitiating the water and weather deities further engendered an occult aspect. Wine was originally used by such peoples as the Romans for sacramental purification of their ships, but on the coming of the religious zealots of the Middle Ages more substantial rites were deemed necessary. Ships were named after saints and their effigies were placed on board: the name 'poop' deck for the after deck is a survival of this old custom, and is taken from the Latin word *puppis* (poop), for the Romans also erected sacred images aboard their ships. Throughout Roman Catholic France in the eighteenth century, the ceremony of launching a ship was almost identical with that of human baptism.

The Norsemen preferred human sacrifice to propitiate the gods when launching a ship. But the custom of breaking a bottle of wine on the bows originated in Georgian days, when a princess of the House of Hanover was asked to sponsor one of the ships of the Royal Navy: the princess threw the bottle with such energy that it nearly decapitated one of the spectators—his claim for damages may still be seen in the Public Records Office in London!

Up to 1690, at all launchings of Royal Navy ships, the health of the ship and her future complement was drunk in wine from a silver cup which was afterwards thrown into the sea. William III (1650-1702) found this practice too expensive when the number of Royal Navy ships increased and he discontinued it. Up to 1811, a Royal Navy ship was always launched by a Royal person, or Dockyard Commissioner. But in that year the Prince Regent (1762-1830), later to become George IV, instituted the custom of asking a woman to perform the office of launching: thus helping to break the stubborn anti-woman taboo (although women

137

were carried—usually as nursing auxiliaries—in Royal Navy men-of-war up to the early 1800s).

Champagne is usually the beverage now utilised to launch ships, but church missionary vessels have been launched with milk. Scotland favours whisky while the Communists shun the capitalist's drink and launch their ships with beer. To make sure that bad luck would not follow the ship she was launching, Miss May Gould, at Boston, Massachusetts, bravely jumped into the water fully clothed and swam after the ship to break the bottle on the bows, when the glass had not broken the first time!

For a long time coins were set by Royal Navy shipbuilders at the step of the mainmast for good luck: reasons for this custom are obscure but Commander Beckett, RN, in his *A Few Naval Customs, Expressions and Traditions* suggests that it is a possible survival of the old Roman custom of placing coins in the mouths of the dead to pay their passage money to Charon when he ferried them across the Styx to Hades' realm.

'Crossing the Line' is an occult custom so old that its exact origin has never been traced. Yet from the early accounts of mariners we know that the Vikings carried out an occult ceremony when crossing certain parallels. Likewise the Phoenicians propitiated the gods at the Pillars of Hercules before venturing out of the Mediterranean into the 'Green Sea of Dark Waters'. Both sets of ceremonial, Viking and Phoenician, probably involved human sacrifice.

Crossing the Tropic of Cancer, crossing the Equator and later the Tropic of Capricorn have all induced sailors to invoke the protection of the nautical gods. By the 17th century the line-crossing ceremonies were of the vaguest sort and are today no more than picturesque customs in the annals of the Royal Navy. In his most interesting volume *Customs and Traditions of the Royal Navy* (Gale & Polden, London 1956) Commander A. B. Campbell, RD, describes one method of 'Crossing the Line' initiation, the relic of a more sinister occult practice:

'Some days before the ship arrives at the Equator a list is made out of members of the ship's company who are crossing the Line for the first time. Meanwhile the boatswain and his mates have been busy making wigs and beards of tow and spun yarn. The sail-maker has been occupied in his spare time in dressing a good-looking young seaman in feminine clothes of dishabille. With wig and showy under-garments this lad will make an amusing show and delight his shipmates. Other members of Neptune's court are also dressed in fancy garb. The "bears" who accompany the court have the job of routing out the uninitiated and bringing them before the monarch.

'Sometimes it is the custom the night before the ship crosses the Line for a messenger from the court of King Neptune to appear on board with a message for the captain, stating at what time the king proposes to board the ship, and presenting the list of those who are to appear before him.

'At noon the next day the boatswain reports to the captain that King Neptune is alongside and would like to pay his respects to him. He would also like to receive tribute from those of his subjects who have not yet paid it. Finally he would like specially to welcome these newcomers to his realm. By this time King Neptune and his wife, surrounded by his courtiers, are waiting on the forecastle. The captain and officers may go forward to greet him or he may be invited to call on the captain. In either case the procession proceeds along the deck to the "throne" which has been erected, the "bears" making horseplay as it progresses. Arriving at the throne, the monarch and his bride take their seats after being regaled with drinks as guests of the captain. Sitting with his trident in his hand King Neptune makes a fine figure, and his spouse keeps the crew in roars of laughter by coquetting with the monarch . . .

. . . 'The first candidate for initiation is then brought before

[Neptune] and interrogated. The king complains that he needs shaving and so he is placed in a chair in front of the king, and the "barber" appears with a bucket of paste or soapsuds and a large wooden razor. Smothering the initiate with this mixture, he proceeds to scrape it off with the blade of his razor. The chair is on a swivel and is placed on the edge of the bath wherein the "bears" are disporting themselves and sousing anyone within reach. The shaving completed to the satisfaction of Neptune the chair is tilted backwards and the initiate tipped into the bath of salt water . . . On completion of the ceremony, the king and his court are refreshed by a glass of grog and prepare to descend to their watery realm.

'In passenger ships today travellers like to be thus initiated, and some liners have beautifully engraved certificates in gold and colour which, duly signed by Neptune and the captain of the ship, are handed to the initiates at dinner that night and are highly prized.'

It is interesting to note how a similar custom is still carried out when airline passengers are given a certificate as they cross the Equator.

Chapter 12

The Occult Way of the Sea

The Fleets set Sail

The precise extent of the sea was never known to the people of ancient civilisations, for their ideas of what lay beyond their own small harbours were based probably on surmise and the many myths passed down from generation to generation. For instance, the people known in the Assyrian texts and the Old Testament as Chaldeans, who inhabited the banks of the Euphrates, the marshland of the Persian gulf and the desert of Arabia, imagined that the earth floated on eternal waters. Furthermore, this raft-earth was thought to be surrounded by a ditch in which a river perpetually flowed. Likewise, the Ancient Egyptians conceived their earth as surrounded by a river on which floated the solar boat carrying the life-giving golden disc of Ra, the sun god.

Neither of these civilisations, however, can be strictly said to have been maritime. Thus, it was not until the coming of the Phoenicians that the great feats of navigation began in ancient history. Few of the Phoenician records have been preserved, but their knowledge of the extent of the oceans was undoubtedly considerable: for instance, they must often have ventured through the Pillars of Hercules to explore the northern coasts of Europe. From their chronicles describing floating seaweed, scholars believe that Phoenician ships may also have sailed as far west as across the Atlantic to the haunted Sargasso Sea, that tangle of deadly weed south of Bermuda.

In the main, the Phoenicians kept their trade routes secret, but some knowledge, however vague, was handed down to the Greeks. 'Oceanus', son of Heaven and Earth, was the name given by the Greeks to an ever-gliding river (*oceanus fluvius*) which they supposed flowed round the earth: for like the Chaldeans and the Ancient Egyptians, the Greeks thought the world was flat. Later the name 'oceanus' was applied to all those waters which lay far outside the sight of land.

By the sixth century BC, Pythagoras the most influential of the early Greek scientists, had computed that the earth was a sphere. And by the time Herodotus (c 485-425 BC), the great Greek historian, came along, man's knowledge of the oceans had greatly increased to include the *Mare Atlanticum*, the *Oceanus Aethiopicus*, the *Mare Australis* and the *Mare Erythraeum*. Herodotus, however, had no knowledge of the seas beyond the European *Mare Cronium*. The third century BC fostered the ideas of the Alexandrian scholar Eratosthenes (276-196) who plotted the parallels of longitude and latitude. Some 70 years later, came the method of map projection of Hipparchus, the Nicaean astronomer.

This ancient era of navigation culminated in the description of the world by Claudius Ptolemaeus, (Ptolemy) (c 90-168 AD), who imagined the *Oceanus Occidentalis* (the Atlantic Ocean off the coast of West Africa) and the *Oceanus Indicus* (Indian Ocean) to be great enclosed seas. He speculated further that if a fleet set sail into the Atlantic from the westernmost point of land, then the countries of the east would very soon be reached.

From the fourth century AD, civilisation suffered greatly at the hands of the barbarian nations, and a mortal blow was dealt to the advancement of navigation and the study of geography. In this age, up to the 15th century, people like Isidore of Seville (with his 'wheel maps') made nonsensical suggestions as to the shape and content of the world. But from this era the occultism of the sea was forged out of the classical myths.

More factual knowledge concerning the sea, however,

received a great impetus from the encouragement of Prince Henry (1395-1460) of Portugal, the son of John I who is popularly known as 'the Navigator'. During Henry's lifetime much of the sea round the coast of Africa, and the eastern parts of the Atlantic, were explored and charted. There followed the great expeditions of Bartholomeu Diaz, Christopher Columbus and Vasco da Gama, but the final link in the knowledge of the great oceans was finally forged when, in September 1513, the Spanish explorer Vasco Nunez de Balbao first caught sight of the Pacific. In 1522 the *Victoria*, commanded by Elcano (part of Magellan's 1519 expedition) reached Spain, having circumnavigated the world. From this time the study of oceanography was taken more seriously, to culminate in the first true oceanographical expedition when Captain James Cook started his voyage of discovery in 1768 aboard the *Endeavour*.

As man's knowledge of the sea grew, his fear of it expanded in direct proportion. So by Captain Cook's time the occult way of the sea had developed into a mystic classification of its own. Occultism and the sea, therefore, began in the mythical age of the gods to solidify into a professional cult, when man was making his most daring exploits in the fields of exploration and maritime industry.

Mythology and the Sea

The Greek word *mythos* formerly meant 'the thing spoken' and concerned speeches or tales. In time *mythos* began to mean a tale or story particularly referring to the various gods and their adventures. Out of this was fostered the idea that man lived in some sort of union with the gods, but on a different plane.

Of the two most widely accepted explanations concerning the evolution of the gods, one states that they were nothing more than supernatural forms built up from the memory or reputation of notable or outstanding men who, when they died, came to be worshipped. This idea, first developed by the fourth century BC Greek scholar Euhemerus, clearly suggests that the worship of ancestors was as well founded in the west as it was in the east. The second explanation is that conceptions about the gods were developed from natural or everyday objects. Be these theories as they may, from the earliest years of man's civilising existence the sea has been given its own group of myths concerning supernatural powers.

Perhaps the most famous of all sea gods was the Greek deity Poseidon, identified by the Romans as Neptune. Derived from a god worshipped by the earliest Aryan invaders of Greece, the Minyans and the Ionians who ingressed around 2000 BC, Poseidon had a varied existence in classical mythology. At first he was probably classed as a sky god and the mate of an earth goddess (who later developed as Demeter, Ceres to the Romans). Certainly he was commonly called (eg, by Homer) 'earth shaker' (*enosichthon* or *ennosigaios*) and was always shown carrying his trident, a three-pronged spear, with which he could shake and shatter whatever he pleased. As he was also thought to have given man the first horse, he was bestowed with a double benefice in mythology:

'Lord Poseidon, from you this pride is ours,
The strong horses, the young horses, and also the rule of
the deep.'

Up to about 1450 BC Poseidon was probably identical with Zeus (Jupiter), who later became supreme ruler among the Greek pantheon of gods. But from the first millenium BC it is probable that Poseidon's pedigree was well established; legends then made him the eldest son of Cronus and Rhea. After the deposition of Cronus, Poseidon and his brothers Zeus and Hades cast lots for sovereignty, the sea becoming Poseidon's share.

After all this Poseidon dwelt in an underwater palace near Aegae in Euboea (but was more often to be found on Mt

Above: According to ancient Egyptian mythology, at sunset on the day he died a man's soul was deemed to board a solar boat to be led through the underworld in the wake of the sun. (*Author's Collection.*)

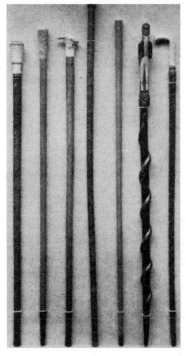

Left: Because of their early connection with magician's wands, walking sticks were popular good luck objects collected by sailors. (*The Victoria & Albert Museum.*)

Below: Ships in bottles were almost universally considered unlucky by sailors. (*Messrs Grugeon, Peterhead.*)

Boats with three sails were considered lucky, probably through some subconscious association with the Trinity. (*Author's Collection.*)

The volcanic isle of Surtsey rose out of the sea in 1963. Such natural phenomena were much feared by sailors. (*The Icelandic Tourist Bureau.*)

Model of Portuguese trawler with eye painted on prow to guard against the ubiquitous 'Evil Eye'. (*Lent to Science Museum, London, by H. C. Bucknall.*)

Figureheads were considered to embody the spirit of the vessel, and thus were the 'heart' of the ship. (*The National Maritime Museum.*)

Hong Kong boatpeople worship at altars during the sea goddess festival. They ask for protection at sea and blessing on their work. (*Hong Kong Tourist Board.*)

Because of the sea's importance in Japan, there are annual sea festivals in their ports and fishing villages. (*Japanese National Tourist Board.*)

Olympus), which is described at the beginning of the *Iliad*. Here he kept his horses with brazen hooves and golden manes, which drew him in his chariot over the sea to make it tranquil. Poseidon's wife was Amphitrite, a granddaughter of the Titan (ie, Elder God) Ocean, lord of the *oceanus fluvius*. Black and white bulls were the main sacrifice to Poseidon.

Both earlier and later civilisations than those of Greece and Rome, of course, had their own sea gods. To the Ancient Egyptians, the sea was only a subsidiary of their cosmos. Thus the benefices of several gods included water and the ocean at large. To some the sea was the 'Lake of Osiris'; Osiris, a god of the earth and vegetation, symbolised in his death the yearly drought and, in his miraculous rebirth, the periodic flooding of the Nile and the growth of grain. Whereas others whose trade it was to fish or sail, might carry the talismans of Sobek for good luck at sea. Sobek was a crocodile-god and was worshipped in cities which depended upon water; such a city was Crocodilopolis, where the reptiles were kept in pools adorned with jewels. Other Ancient Egyptians could very well have related the sea with the witch-god Seth (for his association with storms), or Ptah (who caused all things to be made), or even Anquet, goddess of the third cataract on the Nile.

Among the most interesting Ancient Egyptian sea superstitions was that concerning Abtu and Anet. In Ancient Egyptian myth these were the pair of sacred fish which swam before the solar boat of Ra, the sun god, to whom they gave warning of danger; they were thought also to appear as a warning of the rise of the Nile. Thus, any ship sailing on the Nile, or out at sea, to which two fish attached themselves as 'escorts' (as porpoises do) was considered a very lucky ship indeed.

To the Celts, Llyr was the most important sea deity, and in his entourage were: Addanc (who doubled up in Celtic myth as a dwarf, or marine monster, and dwelt in Lake

Lyon, the 'Lake of Waves'); Adsullata (a water goddess of the Continental Celts); Belisma (a water or river priestess) and Shoney (a British Celtic deity, to whom sacrifices were offered even up to the 1800s, by sailors and fishermen in Eire and on the Island of Lewis). In Celtic myth Dylan, brother of Lleu, was another sea god; personified as the entity Endil, Dylan's memory is extant at St Endellion of the parish of the same name in North Cornwall.

In Norse and Scandinavian sea-lore Aegir and his wife Ran were pre-eminent; Ran was thought to have a palace at Hlesey Island to which she is believed to have taken the souls of drowned sailors. Nehalennia was the sea goddess of the Belgae, or Frisians.

Scandinavian myth has been responsible for a particularly curious sea phantom. Known as Galleytrot in East Anglia, or elsewhere as Black Shuck, Hellblast, Old Snarleyow, Shug Monkey, Padfoot, Trash, Shriker, Hooter or Barguest, this large black sea-born phantom is found in legend from Devon to Yorkshire, and from Cambridge to the Lake District. It derives from the Viking hound of Odin, the mighty dog of war, which is said to have come to British shores when the sea-raiders beached their ships. Two people in particular are on record as having seen the phantom sea-dog. One was marshman and gamekeeper William Fell of Tolleshunt D'Arcy, Essex. He saw the dog 'as big as a calf, with eyes like [bicycle] lamps'; the dog apparently had followed his horse and trap from Peldon along the Wigborough Road to Guisnes Court, where lived his employer Thomas Godfrey Binney, the squire of Tolleshunt D'Arcy.

Mrs A. M. Osborne, the daughter of Squire Binney's gardener, also saw the phantom. She made her sighting at 12.30 am one cold January night while cycling near the spot on the Tollesbury Road known as Jordan's Green. 'The dog . . .' she later wrote to an investigator of psychic phenomena, '. . . had a harsh black coat . . . rough and uncared for . . . its body seemed to stretch the length of my machine . . . its huge tongue looked like bright red velvet . . .'

English historian and antiquary John Stow (c 1525-1605) gives an account of the sea phantom in his famous *Annals*, but of all places Suffolk seems to be richest in tales concerning the phantom. Folk have reported seeing the dog in Leiston churchyard and at Bungay and Blythburgh. To make sure that the phantom sea dog's mystic aura of evil does not pollute consecrated ground, Holy Trinity Church, Blythburgh, proscribes all entry to dogs!

Among the Phoenicians, Asheratian (female) and Bn-Ym, or Khoser-et-Hasis (male) were most important in the myths of Pontus, the sea in Phoenician cosmography. While Ea, or Enki served the Babylonians, and Alaryatis Derketo the Syrians, in many ways El-Khadir, 'the Old Man of the Sea' in Muslim legends and the *Arabian Nights*, resembles El, a god of the north Phoenicians.

In Vedic myth Varuna ruled the sea, but the Polynesians preferred fish gods like Apu-Ko-Hai, or the horrific monster-god Paikea. Njai Loro Kidul, the goddess of the South Sea, is held in great respect by the Javanese. 'Able to fix anything', as the popular Javanese saying describes, the spirit of this sea goddess is particularly strong around Parangtritis, on the Indian Ocean. Here the old Sultans of Jogjakarta once made solemn pilgrimage to commune with the goddess and be refreshed by her philosophy. Of such importance is she still held among the Javanese, that a room with bath is always reserved for her in one of Java's best hotels!

Japanese myth gives sovereignty of the sea to Susa-no-o, Kompira and Benten. Along with Bishamonten, Ebisu, Daikoku, Fukurokuju, Hotei and Jurojin, Benten is one of the *Shichi Fukujin* (the Seven Gods of Luck). The phantom treasure ship of these gods is called *Takarabune* and is supposed to sail into port on New Year's Eve. A picture of the ship bought on New Year's Day and placed under the pillow ensures lucky dreams.

Generally speaking, Kompira, whose shrines are to be found throughout Japan and always in fishing villages and seaports, is the most popular god of Japanese seamen; even though Susa-no-o is a 'creation' god of moon, tide and sea. Kompira's name comes from the Sanskrit *Kumbhira*, the name of the jewelled snake-fish of the River Ganges myths; he is also known as a 'Dragon King of the Sea', who answers the prayers of seamen in distress (also the prayers of farmers petitioning for rain in times of drought). Kompira's principal Shrine is at Kotohira, in Shikoku and all Japanese ships carry a *mamori fuda* (charm) from this shrine. Sometimes sailors and farmers wear such a charm next to the skin.

There are many stories in Japanese mythology told of the miraculous rescues from the sea of pious devotees of Kompira. When passing Kotohira, warships used to cast casks overboard containing coins as an offering from all the members of the crew. These casks were later picked up by the fishermen, who took them to the shrine. At Kotohira is a most interesting collection of sacred objects and Japanese occultism desiderata concerning the sea, and the collection is 'viewed' by thousands of Japanese each year, particularly during the shrine festival on October 10.

For the safety of all Japanese sailors this Kompira folk song is sung by their families:

Kompira fune fune	The boat of the pilgrims to
Oite ni hokakete, shura shu shu	Kompira
Mawareba Shikoku wa Sanshu	With the fair wind rounds
no Nakano Kori	hilly Cape Zozu
Zozu-san Kompira Daigongen	Where is enshrined
	The Great God Kompira

In recent years the seamen and fishermen around the Osaka-Nara-Yokohama-Tokyo coast have tried out different tactics to petition the god's help with modern problems. Following the example of the Kogai Kigyoshu Jusatsu Kitosodan Budhists ('the prayerful band of monks dedicated to imprecating curse and death on polluting industries'), who demonstrated and cursed outside the Yokkaichi chemical plant, they add anti-environmental pollution prayers to the regular petitions to Kompira.

The mystic power of the sea was also recognised in the mythology of the Americas. Here the sea/water deities were almost always female like the Inca Copacti, the Mayan Goddess I, or the delightfully named Aztec goddess of the Jade Petticoat, Chalchihuitlicue, who turned some men into fish so that the waters might be inhabited.

Among the primitive nations of the North American landmass two peoples stand out as having prominent cults of sea occultism: the Eskimo, who inhabit the northern regions from the tip of the Aleutians to Labrador's Goose Bay; and the principal tribes of fishermen, the Haida, Kwakiutle, Tlingit and Tsimshian, who lived along the coast of America, from southern Alaska, through British Columbia and south as far as Oregon.

Eskimo folk-tales hold the cultural position of myths, for there are almost no formalised groups of beliefs about a pantheon of gods. Likewise this folk material is limited by the nature of Eskimo experience. The Eskimo life has always been precarious, so their lives have been dedicated to the successful hunting and the preparation of stores of dried meat in readiness for the time when stocks might not be plentiful. The summer hunting of walrus and whale on the open sea inlets provided much exciting material for adventure tales. But it was the winter periods of waiting for fish and seals at blow holes in the ice which gave rise to the Eskimo occultism of the sea; the many strange stories of ghosts and fantastic spirits which emerge from time to time, the Eskimos say, from the darkness of the sea.

The world of the Eskimo was always filled with mystery. Birds flew away to unknown lands shrieking cries which were taken as presages of good and evil. In the sky the aurora borealis danced, and in these diffuse ribbons of light the Eskimo believed that they saw the images of their dead, to whom they would call out for good luck. The sea itself, the great source of life, was deemed the home of powerful spirits, of whom the ancient fertility mother was the chief. She was known in different areas of the Eskimo lands under different names, but to the Eskimo of the central areas she was Sedna. Sedna became the great mother of all the sea creatures. She it was who caused the storms and migrations of the sea creatures; she it was who controlled the ghosts and spirits of shore and sea, the anonymous number who, because of their deeds, were condemned to walk for ever through the driving snow.

The religious life of the Eskimo centred on the seances at which the *angakok* (shaman) communicated with the spirit world. To help him to 'raise the power', small charms were used like the ivory dolls still to be found round Bank Island.

As far as the Eskimo were concerned any unusual happening or sighting at sea was attributed to wandering ancestral souls or to the spirits of all kinds which daily watched over the people and guarded their welfare.

The fishermen of the north-west coast of America were conditioned over thousands of years to their life of fishing and hunting. Thus, they made full use of their highly specialised natural environment, with its extremes of glacial fiords and scattered islands. Tribal families of these Indians were divided into totemic groups so that one would find Bear people, Killer Whale people, Cannibal Fish Spirit people, Salmon people and so on; each with their own slant on sea occultism.

The mythology of these Indians of the north-west coast of America was slightly more advanced than that of the Eskimo, but there were no clear traces of deities, apart from the Sky Being, the Sun, Moon and the trickster-creator known as the Raven. Most of the ghosts and phantoms of these Indians were half animal and half human, and were particularly aroused should any brave thoughtlessly slaughter animals or fish.

The greatest powers of the sea from ancient times, however, were the spirits of the killer whales, against whom the wraith of the legendary hunter Gunarhnesemgyet was supplicated.

From the fact that many of the world's mythologies gave the sea gods a domain of their own under the ocean, there arose an almost universal superstition that the souls of drowned sailors, or sea-shore dwellers, went down to these domains at death. In American and British sea parlance and lore in particular, such a domain was 'Davy Jones's Locker'. There is considerable doubt about the origin of this phrase, but in general terms it personifies the depths of the sea in their evil aspect as the grave of drowned men. Davy is probably a corruption of Dyved, the fabulous Welshman, or Taffy, or Duffy a West Indian spirit. Jones of course represents Jonah sacrificed to the malevolence of the sea; his 'locker' was the belly of a whale. Others aver that the term derives from Deva Lokka, the Hindu Goddess of Death.

Sailor's Superstitions

From these old myths then, individual superstitions fragmented into complete identities of their own to be disseminated amongst the world's sailors. Sometimes the sailors of one nation might take up the superstitions of another without realising they had done so.

Sailors are perhaps the most superstitious order of workmen in the world. Today the Hindu seaman ranks as the most superstitious of all sailors. Because man has always looked upon the sea in awe, endowing it with supernatural powers and believing it to be subject to the control of nature's more unpredictable laws, sailors down the ages have felt it necessary to call upon some occult protection against evil while at the mercy of the waves.

Fishermen and sailors, for instance, consider it very lucky

to catch fiddle-fish, the slang name for the angel or monk-fish (*Pterophyllum scalare*); its laterally-compressed almost circular body resembling a violin. Although quite inedible, the fish are thought to be good luck to the boat in whose nets they are caught. By tradition they are attached to the ship and towed astern until they finally disintegrate or disappear. On August 5 1949, *The Times* of London reported how fiddle-fish were thus used aboard the Fleetwood trawler *Jamaica*. Some sailors pinned the carcase of a fiddle-fish to their bunks or lockers for more personalised good fortune.

Another fish regarded as auspicious is the porpoise, which must never be harmed. Not only are porpoises said to keep away sharks, but also in 'playing' round ships bring good luck. Long associated with the wind, the gambols of porpoises are often deemed to foretell stormy weather; if the porpoises swim around wildly a storm is thought due, but if they swim sedately through blustery weather, a calm will soon ensue.

Following the example of Admiral Viscount Horatio Nelson (1758-1805) aboard the *Victory*, sailors often nailed horseshoes to masts to avert storms. But a sure way of bringing luck to a sailor was to give him a piece of coal which had come from the sea. The luckiest pieces of coal, of course, were those found at high tide mark, or better still, which had dropped from some ship and had been brought ashore by the tide.

Perhaps the most curious mascot or talisman[1] used by sailors is the hot cross bun. Those tasty cakes, the Christian relics of the small wheaten cakes once eaten at pagan Spring Festivals, have been long associated with magic and the properties of good fortune. Sailors formerly took hot cross

[1]For general aspects of amuletic and talismanic lore see: Brown, Raymond Lamont. *A Book of Superstitions* (David & Charles/Taplinger, 1970) and *A Book of Witchcraft* (1971).

1: The All-Seeing-Eye-of-the-Gods, incorporating the mystic triangle of the Fates; 2: Astarte, Queen of Heaven, basically a fertility goddess; 3: Bes, the bandy-legged demi-god of Egypt. Protection of children at sea; 4: Thor, god of Nordic myth, son of Odin. Good luck against storms at sea; 5: Incorporates the ancient Egyptian symbols Ankh (life) and Utchat (health); 6: A pre-Columbian figurine for protection while fishing; 7: The ancient Egyptian solar discs, entwined cobras and ankh symbol—a powerful amulet against evil spirits; 8: Bast, the ancient Egyptian fire and cat goddess of Bubastis. Protection against fire at sea; 9: Horned skipper of the Skidbladnir, in Nordic myth the ship of Frey, son of Njord and Skadi.

buns aboard ship to prevent shipwrecks, but one widow used them to try to bring her sailor son safely home.

Around 1825, the then licensee of the inn later called *The Widow's Son* in Devons Road, Bow, London, had a son serving at sea. Every year, should the son be still at sea on Good Friday, the old lady placed a hot cross bun aside against his safe return. At length however, the young man was lost at sea, but the old lady continued to add each Good Friday a hot cross bun to the mouldering collection which she hung in a basket in her bar-parlour. Long after the old lady's death the custom was continued. Each year a sailor was invited to hang up ceremonially a new hot cross bun above the bar and place the year old one in a basket likewise suspended nearby; his fee for the task was free beer.

There were, of course, several mystic or semi-religious rituals a family could re-enact to assure the safety of their loved-ones at sea. One of the rituals was for children to chant this rhyme as a 'kiss blessing':
'I see the moon and the moon sees me,
God bless our (father) on the sea.'
After the chant the children blew a kiss to him out to sea. In Somerset, however, a rhyme was said and an apple thrown into the Bristol Channel:
'Come high tide or low tide
   Whatever it be.
Oh God bring my father
   Home safely to me.'

Small dried branches of seaweed, known as 'lady's trees' were often to be seen in sailors' cottages. Either hanging above the hearth, or set in vases on the mantlepiece, the trees were thought to protect the sailor's house as well as his person while he was away at sea.

Most sailors' superstitions, however, are connected with omens and taboo. Omens, the signs and forewarnings by which sailors claim to know if such-and-such occurs so-and-so will follow, are the objects of a belief based on a predetermined future, totally fatalistic; that a specific cause will always, automatically bring about a specific effect. While taboos (don't speak certain words, or commit certain actions, otherwise disaster will befall you) are forbidden because they are deemed to arouse ghosts, evil spirits, or the in-human magical 'essence' that pervades every aspect of primitive thought, to assault the trespasser.

Sailors generally avoid mentioning by name eggs, rabbits, and knives while on board ship; sometimes, however, knives were thrust into the masts of fishing boats for luck, especially the ships of deep-sea fishermen. Further, cargoes of pigs, dogs and horses are commonly considered unlucky; aboard American ships cats are thought creatures of ill-omen. Among American sailors these were the most com-mon cat superstitions: should cats frolic aboard a ship this was thought a sure sign of a storm. Should cats wash behind their ears this would bring rain. But, the worst omen of all was that should a cat be seen climbing the rigging the ship was doomed!

Black objects are also avoided on ships, and swearing, up-turned shoes or seaboots, reversed maps, pins, umbrellas, ladders, playing cards, whistling and pieces of cut hair and fingernails have all been taboo at one time or another. In the north of Scotland it was believed that no man should put to sea if his hair clippings would not burn when thrown on the household fire. But no woman should likewise attempt to burn her hair clippings when any of her blood relatives were at sea; if she did so they were doomed to drown.

In the sailors' mess the ringing of a glass was thought to foretell the death of a comrade, and must be stopped im-mediately. It was said, rather churlishly, that if this was done then the devil would 'take two soldiers in lieu'. The evil aspect of death could be avoided, the wise said, if the glass was struck an odd number of times. In the navies of the world odd numbers are considered lucky and have been so from the time of the great Roman epic poet Publius Vergilius Maro (70-19 BC).

For their omens of ensuing danger Malayan seamen observe the actions of frogs. 'Wars' among frogs are not uncommon in Malaysia, and zoologists theorise that the frogs, which furiously hop around and bite each other, are doing so to stake personal mating grounds. To the superstitious Malayan seamen and fishermen, however, the frog 'wars' are portents of individual and national disaster. Soon after a particularly vicious frog 'war', the cult devotees point out, the Japanese invaded and occupied Malaya from initial landings at Kota Bharu on December 8 1941. Again the country's 12-year struggle against Communist terrorists began after Kedah frogs warred in 1948. Likewise before the violent race riots which erupted in Kuala Lumpur in 1969, there had been a furious frog battle near Penang.

In November 1970 a frog fight broke out on a rubber plantation near Sungei Siput (100 miles north-east of Kuala Lumpur) and the local astrologers and *bomohs* (witch doctors) predicted more troubles for Malaysia, with 'water borne' people being in particular danger. True to their predictions, in early January 1971 monsoon rains poured down on Malaysia causing widespread flooding, the worst in the country's history. With some 200,000 threatened with starvation and drowning, Malaysia's Prime Minister Tun Abdul Razak declared a situation of national disaster. For weeks afterwards no Malaysian seaman or fisherman set sail without first consulting a soothsayer.

Rats and sharks have long been held to presage disaster and sailors commonly dislike carrying a corpse on or off a ship. Generally those who die on board ship are buried at sea. But should it be absolutely necessary to bring a cadaver home, then the superstitious say it must lie athwart the ship and never 'end on'. When home port is reached, the corpse must leave the ship before members of the crew do so.

The 'Ship Wrecker'

The mystic influence of one corpse in particular is thought to have caused several ships to flounder. Sir Ernest Alfred Wallis Budge (1857-1934) was one of the greatest Egyptologists of all time. He was a distinguished archaeologist and conducted many excavations in Mesopotamia and Egypt. From 1893 to 1924, Budge was Keeper of the Egyptian and Assyrian Antiquities at the British Museum. Although a scholar of note, Sir Ernest had a fanciful turn of mind and one of his famous stories concerned a mummy-case[2] which was sometimes euphemistically called 'The Ship Wrecker'.

Sometime in the 1880s, recounted Sir Ernest, an Arab living in a mud-walled village near the gigantic ruined city of Thebes (now in the upper part of the United Arab Republic), sold a mummy-case to three Englishmen. Ignoring the popular superstition thereabouts that it was unlucky to disturb the bodies and coffins of dead Ancient Egyptians, the Englishmen set out for Cairo with the mummy-case stowed in their luggage.

On their way to Cairo the Englishmen apparently stopped off to do some duck-shooting, and one day one of their number had his arm shattered when his shotgun exploded. Another of the three men mysteriously disappeared from the party and was never seen again (it was presumed that he had fallen overboard!). Fearing that the mummy-case was truly haunted with evil, the third Englishman is thought to have sold the coffin in Cairo.

All first three owners of the mummy-case died in mysterious circumstances. Sometime around 1888 the case came into the possession of a rich Streatham (London) collector of Ancient Egyptian antiquities. Here the case was seen by the famous mystic, Madam Helena Petrovna Blavatsky (1831-

---

[2]British Museum Exhibit 22542, Case 35, marked: 'Mummy cover from the coffin of an unknown princess from Thebes, XXI Dynasty. About 1050 BC. Presented A. F. Wheeler, 1889'.

91), co-founder of the Theosophical Society with Colonel H. S. Olcott in 1875, who advised that the funerary relic be disposed of, warning: 'Get rid of it or it will kill you'.

Shortly afterwards the Streatham collector did sell the case, this time to an antiquary who decided to have it photographed. The photographer died the next day. Messrs W. A. Mansell & Co, the famous Oxford Street photographers were then commissioned to photograph the case. In an interview in 1904 with a reporter from the *Morning Leader*, the principal of the photographic firm, Mr Mansell, explained how a series of disasters followed the commission.

Mr Mansell's son and an assistant first went to see how best to photograph the case. At the premises of the antiquarian they arranged the mummy-case in the best possible photographic position and planned to return the next day to photograph it. On his way home that evening, young Mansell smashed his thumb in a railway carriage door. Further, the assistant found, when he had arrived home, that one of his children had been badly cut by falling into a cucumber frame. Next morning the same assistant gashed his face as he was adjusting the camera to photograph the mummy-case.

Eventually the case was successfully photographed. When developed, however, the print did not show the face of the 3,000-year old Egyptian princess depicted on the mummy-case, but the livid, vile face of a dark-eyed venomous old woman!

Instantly the owner sold the case to a female antiquary. The morning after it had been delivered, the woman found when she came down to breakfast that every bit of glass and china in the house had been mysteriously smashed. Thereafter the mummy-case was credited with poltergeist powers and was re-sold. The case now passed to a Mr A. F. Wheeler, who presented it to the British Museum in 1889. Of the two porters who carried the case into the Museum, one slipped and broke his leg and the other died suddenly soon after!

By this time the tales of the supposed mystic power of the mummy-case began to spread. It was rumoured that Sir Ernest Budge took the mummy out of its case and sold it to a Canadian who put it aboard the *Empress of Ireland*, which sank a few days later. The mummy floated, the gossips said, and was later picked up. Perhaps the most absurd story was that the influence of the mummy caused the loss of *HMS Hampshire* in which Field-Marshal Earl Kitchener of Khartoum (1850-1916) was sailing. (The *Titanic* disaster was also blamed on the mummy by some.)

Eventually Sir Ernest issued a statement that the mummy-case had not been sold by the British Museum, nor was ever likely to be! Yet Sir Ernest was later quoted as saying enigmatically: 'Never print what I say in my lifetime, but that mummy-case caused the War!' (ie, World War I). Incidentally, in 1966 the Director of Egyptian Antiquities in Cairo reluctantly agreed to let some of pharaoh Tutankhamun's treasures be shipped to Paris (see: *A Book of Witchcraft*). He was killed in a car accident shortly afterwards.

Some of the sailors of the older generation still look for omens in the colours of the sea. To the human eye, the most obvious patterning of surface water is indicated by colour. The deep blue water of the open sea is the colour of emptiness and barrenness, while the green water of coastal areas is the colour of life.

Sea water appears blue because the sunlight is reflected back to the eyes from the water molecules, or from very minute particles suspended in the sea. As the light rays penetrate deep water, all the red rays and most of the yellow rays of the spectrum are absorbed, so that when the light returns to the eyes it is chiefly the cool blue rays which are seen.

The yellow, brown and green hues of coastal waters are derived from the minute algae and other micro-organisms so abundant there. Seasonal abundance of certain forms containing reddish or brown pigments may cause the 'red

Top right: *Umi Bozu, the giant ghostly Sea Priest, or Monk, who rises from the depths to frighten seamen; as portrayed in the c1845 Ukiyoye style by artist Kuniyoshi (1798-1861), in his* Tokaido go-ju-san tsui (*Pairs to the 53 stations of the Tokaido*). (The Victoria & Albert Museum. Crown Copyright.)

Although it is a debatable point amongst scholars, the Umi Bozu could be said to be identical with the shojo. These are Japanese marine spirits, who in myth are great drinkers and revellers. In Japanese art they are usually shown with huge sake (rice wine) jars, or cups and dippers, and may be represented dancing on the waves. Shojo are considered quite innocuous to mortals, who try to trap them using sake as bait. The Umi Bozu is usually shown with a black outline and shaven head, while the shojo have vivid red hair (from which, say the old texts, red dye can be extracted should you be cunning enough to trap a shojo).

Bottom right: *The* ama *diver carries off one of the Jewels of the Sea from the Dragon King's palace, chased by his retainers in this triptych print by Kuniyoshi, 1847-48.* (The Victoria & Albert Museum. Crown Copyright.)

In the popular Japanese tale, immortalised by Madame Yei Ozaki, the Dragon King stole the famous Crystal of Buddha, in which could be seen the image of Buddha riding on a white elephant. Risking her life, an ama girl diver swam down to the Dragon King's lair and brought back the Crystal concealed in a self-inflicted wound. The temple of Shidoji, Shido-no-ura, is dedicated to her memory.

From early times the Japanese considered the landmass under the sea to be a separate mythical kingdom, ruled by the Dragon King of Dragons, whose daughter was able to transform herself into a beautiful mortal woman. In this guise, for instance, she appears in the classic story of the fisherman Urashima Taro, who ultimately married her. The goddess Benten is thought to be the daughter of the Dragon King when in his human-like form. The Dragon King is known as Ryujin, Ryujin Sama, and Ryuo Kyo, and his palace as Ryugu. His chief assistant carries the tama, *the Tide-Riding-Jewel, the spiritual essence of the universe.*

164

On Ascension Day each year, the Doge of Venice symbolically 'married' the sea. This custom was based on the old pagan idea that the sea was a Great Mother who must be annually propitiated. Throwing a gold ring into the Adriatic, the Doge recited: 'We wed thee, O sea, in token of perpetual domination'. This was deemed to bring good luck and prosperity to Venice for a whole year. In this painting by Antonio Canale (called Canaletto, 1697-1768), the Doge's state galley *Bucentaur* returns to the mole of Venice. (*Dulwich College Picture Gallery.*)

Top left: *The ghost of the Emperor Sutoku* (1124-41) *races across the surface of the sea from his rock of exile in this print by Kuniyoshi* (*published c*1840 *in the series* Hyaku-nin isshu no uchi (*The Hundred Poets*), *for which Kuniyoshi took his inspiration from scenes of court life in the Fujiwara period.* (The Victoria & Albert Museum. Crown Copyright.)

Bottom left: *Here the* Shichi Fukujin, *Seven Gods of Good Luck, sail in their boat* Takarabune, *with sacred Mount Fuji in the background. Very lucky emblems for sailors, the names of the* Shichi Fukujin *are:* Bishamonten, *the God of Riches, who is also one of the* Shitenno, *the Four Buddhist Kings of Heaven;* Benten, *Goddess of Music, Eloquence, Arts and Fortune. Thought by some to be daughter of the Dragon King of the sea, she is particularly worshipped by mariners and fishermen at the Japanese island of Enoshima, near Kamakura, and at Chikubushima on Lake Biwa.* Ebisu, *God of Food and Honest Dealing, patron of fishermen; he usually carries a fishing rod and a large* tai *fish under his arm.* Daikoku, *a good luck bringer, carries a sack of precious gifts and holds a hammer in his right hand.* Fukurokuju, *the God of Longevity.* Jurojin, *the aged scholar. And* Hotei, *the obese God of Plenty.*

A picture of the Takarabune *bought on New Year's Day and placed under the pillow is deemed to ensure lucky dreams.* (The Victoria & Albert Museum. Crown Copyright).

water' known from Biblical times. So common is this condition in some enclosed waters that they owe their names to it, the Red Sea and the Vermilion Sea being examples.

The colours of the sea are only indirect signs of the presence, or absence of conditions needed to support surface life. What largely determines where marine creatures live, however, is the food content of the water: particles of this food often being invisible to the human eye. The sea is by no means a uniform solution of water, parts of it are more salty than others, and other sections are warmer or cooler. The Pacific, being the deepest of the oceans, is usually observed as dark blue.

In the main, the sailors of ancient times looked upon blue sea as lucky and green as unlucky, for any hue reminiscent of plankton was a reminder of the ill-fated ships marooned in the much feared Sargasso Sea.

Black patches in the sea were thought of as supernatural 'evil islands', while red tints meant some sort of imminent violence. Yellow, however, was considered ambivalent when occurring in sea water. As the hue of the sun and gold, yellow represented perfection, but in earlier times saffron-yellow suggested a treacherous spirit. This latter probably stemmed from the customs of clerics wearing yellow vestments on Good Friday, as a reminder of the Jew's vindictiveness in crucifying Jesus Christ.

Sailors from Port Mahomack in the north of Scotland look upon white as a colour of ill omen. Thus, sailors must be sure that no white stones are on board, even among the ballast. Blue, however, is lucky among these sailors and should a member of a ship's crew die, the ship would have a blue 'mourning' line painted round her.

Port Mahomack mariners and the sailors along the Ross and Cromarty, Inverness, Nairn, Moray and Banff coasts, have evolved their own brand of superstition. Hereabouts it is thought unwise to turn a boat anti-clockwise; should you do so 'she may be smashed on the hidden rocks of the sea'. Worse still, of course, was to turn widdershins, which put your ship in the power of the Devil. It was believed in these parts that the souls of dispossessed sailors or sea phantoms would seize the prow of a ship in a storm and try and turn her away from the sun so as to put the crew outside God's protection. Likewise, no boat-builder thereabouts would use rowan wood to make anything on board if he had also used juniper. For these two woods were deemed to have a mystic 'hate' between them. He was careful also that no haunted tree, the home of a ghost or spirit, was used in the building of a ship, for the ghost would thus come to sea with its tree (cf, witches and trees in *A Book of Superstitions* and *A Book of Witchcraft*). 'The boat-builder who knows his trade must place a crooked sixpence in the keel of every boat, runs a local superstition; this action was intended to avert evil through jealousy. Further, planks, nets and so on should always be let down from the right-hand side for a good catch and good luck, say folk around Port Mahomack, for that is what St Peter always did!

Among the birds considered of ill-omen amongst sailors the albatross (see: *A Book of Superstitions*) and the raven are pre-eminent. Only one bird, the kingfisher, really evoked any feelings of *camaraderie* among sailors and fishermen. Sacred to the peoples of many past civilisations, and famous in the Greek legend of Halcyone, wife of Ceyx, King of Trachis, the kingfisher is thought to bring good weather. Sailors believe that if the feathers, or pieces of carcass of a kingfisher are hung somewhere on the ship, then they will always show in which direction the wind is blowing by turning towards it. Even though the famous London physician and antiquary, Sir Thomas Browne (1605-82) experimented thus with carcasses of two kingfishers aboard a ship and found that they actually turned away from the wind, the discovery had no effect on the general belief.

Strangely enough, a bee found aboard ship while at sea is

considered the best of good omens, particularly by sailors from East Anglia. Sailors still fear bad luck on a voyage should they happen to meet certain people before boarding the ship. Among these so-called unlucky people are lawyers, tailors, dressmakers and clergymen. Anyone mentally defective, or cross-eyed is similarly feared.

Women attempting to board a ship before it sails is a particularly strong taboo and ranks perhaps as the strongest held of all superstitions of the sea. Maggie Theaker, a 70-year-old Straithes (Whitby, Yorkshire) woman testified how few sailors would set sail around the Yorkshire coast if the first person they saw before embarking was a woman. It is the general belief of fishermen all round the British Isles that it is unlucky to take a woman to the fishing grounds. In 1955 the English folklorist Ruth L. Tongue (see: Briggs, Katherine M. and Tongue, Ruth L. *Folktales of England*. Routledge & Keegan Paul/University of Chicago Press 1965) collected this story concerning the women taboo from N. Marchant, 12, daughter of a lightship sailor from Harwich:

'There was a gentleman had a beautiful daughter who was bad at heart, and they said she knew more than a Christian should, and they wanted to swim her [ie, *iudicium aquae*: ordeal by immersion in water to determine her guilty or innocent of witchcraft; a common but strictly non-official anti-witch practice in England, Scotland, Germany and America], but no one dared because of her father. She drew a spell on a poor fisherman, and he followed for love of her wherever she went. He deserted his troth-plight maid, though he was to be married in a week, and he ran away to sea with the gentleman's daughter and unbeknown to all the rest [ie, of the fleet] took her out with them to the fishing . . .

'A storm blew up and the whole fishing fleet were lost to a man for they had on board a woman with them at sea, though none knew of it but her lover. It was she that had whistled up the storm that had drowned her own lover, for she hated everyone. She was turned into a four-eyed cat, and ever after she haunted the fishing fleet.

'So that it is why even now fishermen won't cast their nets before half-past three (cock-crow)—my uncles won't—and they always throw a bit back into the sea for the cat.'

According to European sea-lore, no ship should set sail on Candlemas Day (February 2), the first Monday in April (generally held as the birthday of the Old Testament murderer Cain), nor on December 31, when Judas Iscariot is thought to have hanged himself. Any Friday was also considered unlucky. Consequently no superstitious sailor would sail a ship which had had its keel laid on a Friday. This Friday superstition can be traced back to the days of the Norsemen, for Friday is the day named after the goddess Frega, the dispenser of ill-luck in Norse mythology.

Surprisingly enough, it is thought unlucky to quote passages from the Bible while on board ship, except of course during burial at sea; the most feared Bible quotation being Psalm 109. Called 'The Cursing Psalm', according to legend it was the recital of this psalm by a sailor unjustly condemned to death in 1707, which led to the wreck of three ships off the Scillies, including the flagship *HMS Association* of Admiral Sir Cloudesley Shovel (1650-1707). A native of the Scillies, the sailor had apparently warned the Admiral of the dangerous rocks nearby. The Admiral had taken offence at the seaman's temerity and ordered him to be hanged. With the rope round his neck the seaman had cursed the Admiral and his fleet with a parody of Psalm 109. 'May his children be fatherless and his wife a widow . . . May his prosperity be cut off; may his name be blotted out in the second generation . . . For he did not remember to show kindness but pursued the poor and needy'. Soon afterwards the ships were wrecked.

The curse was further fulfilled in a bizarre fashion. Sir Cloudesley's body, washed ashore a few hours after the wreck of the *Association*, was despatched and buried, by a gipsy woman avid for the valuable emerald ring which she noticed on his finger. She confessed the truth many years later on her own deathbed. The story and superstition was recalled when frogmen-divers recently recovered treasure from the wreck of Sir Cloudesley's flagship.

Once the idea of the omen had been well established in popular belief, it was only a matter of time before mysterious happenings at sea were automatically linked with the occult. Ships lost in stormy weather were often deemed to reappear as omens against bad weather. Here are some examples.

Rough seas are to be expected if the phantom ship called *Packet Light*, which still haunts the Gulf of St Lawrence, appears; the ghostly origin of this ship being in its wrecking during a storm near Prince Edward Island sometime during the 1880s. At San Francisco the Cape Horner *Tennessee*, a goldrush clipper, appears when mists are thick near the Golden Gate Bridge. As the mists clear the ship is said to disappear into a blue-grey haze. The Belgian ship *Concordia* and the Latin-American *La Plata* are also 'weather ghosts' which ply the North Sea and Atlantic Oceans respectively. Weather ghosts of course need not be in the form of phantom ships. Some are in human shape, but with some connection with the sea, like the ghost of the demented Southwold (Sussex, England) woman who threw herself off the neighbouring North Pier, when she heard that her husband had been drowned at sea.

Some Modern Uses of Traditional Superstitions

It is interesting to note how the old marine superstitions have been taken up, for instance by the modern frogman diver. A recent survey showed that many of the above-mentioned omens and occult signs are still believed by divers (on both sides of the Atlantic) today. Mr MacJohns, a young Devonshire-born diver, runs a boat out of Penzance, Cornwall, every morning. Although not a religious man,

MacJohns does follow the old Devonshire superstition of never putting to sea on a Sunday. In a recent interview he explained why:

'I never go out on Sundays although the money for the lobsters and crayfish during the tourist season is excellent. When I first started diving for lobsters, I had an old local who looked after the boat, and he was terrified at the thought of putting to sea on a Sunday, even if the sea was flat calm. He said that local belief held that if you fished on a Sunday, you would lose ten times the value of what you had gained. I'm not religious, but we did in fact lose valuable gear while fishing off Sennen Cove, near Land's End, one Sunday, which rather deterred me from putting to sea on that day again.

'But a couple of weeks later, Pete, one of our most experienced divers, insisted that we go out. The weather was beautiful, and he said it was silly to lose money through a whim. So we put out, and Pete, who is an atheist, had a terrible dive. It was in fairly shallow water, about 60 feet, so there was no question of hallucination through depth, and we later checked his oxygen bottles and found that they were working perfectly. And, of course, he was dead sober—no sensible diver would enter the water with so much as a vague hangover.

'Anyway he went down and five minutes later he surfaced and said: "For God's sake let's get out of here". He'd apparently seen all sorts of things. As he went down he felt that he was being followed, and started to hear voices muttering. When he reached the bottom, he saw a gigantic figure lying on the sand—the area was very clear—which vanished as he approached. Then he said he felt he was surrounded by unseen presences who wanted to hold him there and rip his air-pipe out of his mouth. So he came up pretty quickly. I've never seen him so scared, and he said he'd never had an experience remotely like it in the ten years' diving.'

The Religious Approach

Sometimes the deeds of religious figures, like saints and clerics, were woven into the occultism of the sea. Such was the case with St Elmo. St Elmo's fire is the name usually given by sailors to the bright, glowing light—caused by an electrical discharge during storms—which often appears on the masts and yards of ships. Legend connects it with St Elmo, the patron saint of Mediterranean seamen. St Elmo is said to have died at sea during a severe storm. In his last few moments, St Elmo is reported to have promised the crew that he would return and show himself in some occult form if they were destined to survive the storm. Shortly after he died, a strange light appeared at the masthead and this occurrence was assumed to be the saint's occult sign.

The Greeks and Romans both knew of this natural phenomenon and called it 'Helen' after the sister of the Divine Twins, Castor and Pollux. Such an idea may be compared with the 'St Helena's Fire' of the Christian Greeks and the mystic *Corpus Santo* of the Spanish and Portuguese seamen.

As the phenomenon usually occurs when the worst of a storm is over, sailors generally look upon it as a good sign, as the English navigator, buccaneer and hydrographer William Dampier (1652-1715) recorded in his *Voyages and Descriptions* (1690):

'Towards late in the day thunder and rain abated, and then we clearly saw a Corpus Sant at our mainmast head on the very top of the truck. The sight rejoiced our crew exceedingly for the worst of any storm is commonly believed over when the Corpus Sant is seen aloft, but when it can be seen clearly from the deck it is accounted an evil omen, a bad sign.'

Christopher Columbus (c 1446-1506), the famous Italian navigator, is noted as having used the St Elmo's fire phenomenon as a religio-psychological doctrine to cheer his disgruntled crew.

Some historians believe that St Elmo's fire was the basis

and logical explanation for this following famous sea phantom sighting. The 800-ton *Palatine* was a Dutch-owned vessel bound from Amsterdam to Philadelphia, Pennsylvania, with 304 emigrants aboard. In her early days the *Palatine* had been a fine ship, trading round the Levant carrying French and Spanish goods. But in the year of her disaster, 1752, she had deteriorated so much that the old seamen watching her load at Amsterdam said they could even smell the rot eating through her planking.

Palatine's crew was equally disreputable and her captain a drunken scoundrel. Because of the *Palatine's* lack of facilities, disease coupled with the arduous 3,000-mile crossing always took its toll of the passengers. This suited the captain, of course, for he had the privilege of first pickings among the personal possessions of any emigrant who died aboard his ship. Consequently he was not against murdering a few of his passengers for personal gain.

From the first hours of her last voyage the *Palatine's* fate was settled. The ship always made landfall off Block Island, on Long Island Sound, between Montauk Point and Martha's Vineyard. Block Island had a sinister reputation, for here the motley collection of farmer and fishermen inhabitants supplemented their sparse incomes by wrecking.

At the end of his previous voyage the captain of the *Palatine* had arranged with the wreckers that he would drive the *Palatine* ashore at Block Island. The passengers who had survived the trip from Amsterdam would then be murdered and their possessions and the ship's cargo be shared among the wreckers, captain and crew. This plot, however, did not go precisely to plan.

When the *Palatine* set sail on her last fateful journey the weather held good, and the ship's patched canvas set her west-ward at a steady clip. Soon, however, the weather broke and badly buffeted the ship, which thereafter made slow headway. On the 19th day out of Amsterdam the captain's greed got the better of him, and he had all the passengers lined up on deck and on the struts of the barnlike travelling compartment below. After being systematically searched the passengers were robbed: those who resisted were murdered and their bodies tossed into the sea. For some two more months the cold and hungry passengers somehow lasted out until the coast of Rhode Island was finally sighted.

By this time it is probable, for records of the *Palatine* story are conflicting, that the ship's crew mutinied and murdered their captain. Taking the plunder they had looted from the passengers, the crew took to the boats, leaving the hapless emigrants to drift at the mercy of the elements. The *Palatine*, however, remained on her crash course and ran aground on Block Island, sometime between December 25 1752 and January 1 1753.

After stripping the *Palatine* of all worthwhile plunder, the Block Island wreckers set fire to the ship. Again the records are conflicting; one set says that the wreckers murdered the passengers, while another states that the surviving passengers were rescued and well cared for. As the schooner drifted out to sea ablaze from stem to stern, the watchers on the shore saw a terrifying sight. Drawing her stricken body through the inferno of flame, a woman was seen on the *Palatine's* deck, and across the water came the sound of her parched voice screaming the name of a child. Agonising moments later the woman vanished as the flames surged higher. By morning all traces of the *Palatine* had disappeared, but the people of Block Island long remembered the demented woman in the flames and the sound of her voice screaming for her child.

During the early days of January 1754, the wraith of the *Palatine*, still blazing, was reported as being seen off Block Island, with the woman's voice clearly heard again above the roar of the sea. In later years the phantom of the *Palatine* was supposedly sighted off Rhode Island several times, by men like Captain John Collins of the Dramatic Line packet

Roscius; by Captain Asa Eldridge of the *Pacific*; by Captain Samuels of the pacemaker *Dreadnought*, and by the captain and crew of the New Bedford whaler *Montreal*. Each believed that they had seen the *Palatine* at the time and thought the sighting important enough to report in their logs.

Fire-ships often figure prominently in north-European folklore and, of these, two are important as mythological phantoms. Manannán, the sea god, mentioned in Alexander Carmichael's *Carmina Gadelica*, is believed to sail his phantom fire galley, 'Wave Sweeper', once every seven years from the Isle of Man to the Hebrides. Some say that he is inspecting his kingdom, but others aver that he is on his way to Tir-nan-Og (the mystic land of eternal youth); still more, romantically believe that Manannán is making a visitation to collect the spirits of the good men who have died, to convey them out into the western sea where lies the Celtic Paradise.

Kenneth Macleod in his charming *The Celt and the Sea* tells of the second famous phantom fire-ship. The 'long-theine' is regularly seen by the 'gifted ones' off the Isle of Eigg (the inner Hebridean island which must never be mentioned by name at sea; instead it should be called Nem-Ban-More, 'The Island of Big Women'). The phantom ship careers past the island at lightning speed, 'and on deck was a long, lean black creature, with a fiddle in his hand, and he ever playing and dancing and laughing . . . awful was the howling that was below . . . Doubtless the fire-ship was conveying the soul of some unrighteous Southern Lord to [hell]'.

A Cult of Sea Monsters

There are certainly more things in the oceans of the world than are dreamt of by zoologists and marine biologists, if at least, sailors' tales of giant worms and monster tadpoles are to be believed. Down the centuries countless generations of

The Seven Sea Monsters Most Feared by Medieval Sailors

B C

The Kraken

The Man-eating Sea Serpent

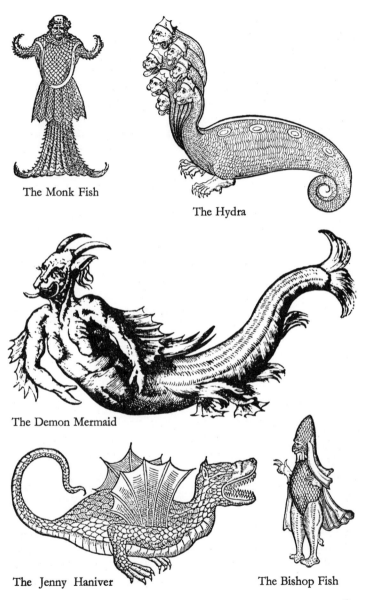

The Monk Fish

The Hydra

The Demon Mermaid

The Jenny Haniver

The Bishop Fish

mariners have actually believed in fabulous sea beasts. So much so that an entire occult cult arose round them. In this cult the following monsters were classed as the most important.

A strange superstition which lasted for many centuries, was the belief that the 'sucking fish', or remora, could hinder and arrest the progress of a ship under full sail, by attaching its tail to a rock, and by seizing the keel of the ship in its mouth. The remora legend was mentioned by Philip Massinger (1583-1640) in his *Renegado*, by Edmund Spencer (c 1552-99) in his *Visions of the World's Vanity*, by François Rabelais (c 1495-1553) in the fourth book of his *Gargantua and Pantagruel* and by Pliny, who tells a vivid story of how such a sea monster attacked the imperial bark of Caius Caligula.

Olaus Magnus, in his *Historia de Gentibus Septentrionalibus* (Basle 1567) gives testimony concerning the Great Norwegian Sea Serpent, which echoed the earliest known sea serpent of Aristotle's *De Generatione Animalum* (Venice 1526). While the perennial sea serpent with armour-tough scales and coiled tail is common in the sea-lore of most cultures, the Norwegians seem to have taken the beast as their own national marine symbol; at least if one is to believe such testimony, attributed to Archbishop Hans Agede, as quoted in Erich Pontoppidan's (Bishop of Bergen) sterling work *The Natural History of Norway* (London 1755).

Another gigantic animal of Scandinavian sea legend was the kraken, said by some to resemble an island when it surfaced (Olaus Wormius in *Antiquitates Donicae* 1643-51, describes it as *similiorum insulae quam bestiae*). The kraken was the most feared sea beast, for on its skin there was thought to dwell all manner of underwater demons.

The hydra, the many-headed serpent of classical legend, the monk-fish, the bishop-fish and demon mermaid, are all based on sailors' mis-sightings, or errors of identification; but the 'Jenny Haniver' sea monster is purely a fabrication of man's imagination. Basically this monster was made up of a dragon's head, wings and body, and a serpent's tail, all supported on huge four-clawed feet. This monster is mentioned both by Ulisse Aldrovandi in his *Historia Monstrorum* (Bologna 1642) and by Konrad Gesner in his *Historia Animalum* (London 1551-87), who gullibly classed the phoney beast under the general title of 'dragons'. Fake monsters like these latter were 'made' (usually from fish tails and monkey heads) by the natives of many East Indian Islands and the fishermen of Japan.

To protect themselves against sea monsters and any 'magic' powers which these monsters might possess, sailors bought all kinds of charms like pieces of carved horn (South England, Norway, Denmark), slivers of slate (East America, Sweden, North Scotland), sugared skulls (Mexico), horse figures (China), dried apples (Yorkshire coast, Somerset), ashes—human and animal—in a box (Africa), wooden images of barnacle geese (Ireland), carved wooden and ivory images of saints (France, Spain, Portugal, Italy), pieces of bat wing (East Europe, America), fragments of bone (Americas, Japan, Norway, Scotland, Africa) and so on. Others had charms like crucifixes, or 'lucky' stars and anchors tattooed on their arms. American navy men had the names of 'lucky' ports and zodiac signs tattooed on arms and legs.

The Americas have long been considered the domicile of eccentric monsters and sea beasts of all kinds, like the huge monster believed to live off Cape Anne, Boston, Massachusetts and the 'upright standing whales' of New England. In 1817 a sensation was created among the Massachusetts fisherfolk by the presence of what was apparently a sea monster 'of immense size' and 'wonderful rapidity'. Until well into the 1900s, sea monsters from the primeval depths continued to terrorise the coastal regions of North America as well as the inland waters. During the 1930s 'a huge grey thing' once emerged from the 60 ft deep river at Newport,

Arkansas, bringing hordes of sightseers into the area. Scotland's Loch Ness Monster is as useful to the Scottish Tourist Board as this latter monster was to the Arkansas Department of Tourism!

Again in 1931 an 18 ft long 'marine monster' was captured at Sandusky, Ohio and was put on view by two enterprising businessmen. Most astonishing of all, however, was the gigantic phallus-headed horror which protruded its bulk above the waves for long enough to be photographed off San Diego Bay. Still more feared is the monster in Cadbury Bay, near Victoria, Canada, whose nocturnal moans are still reported.

Even today, as men walk on the surface of the moon, mankind is unwilling to abandon the beliefs in the occult way of the sea, even to believing in sea monsters whose shape represents to many all the evil mystique of the sea.

Unscrupulous Use of Marine Occultism

Superstition, belief in sea monsters and the fear of sea phantoms, have all been used by seamen for their own ends: particularly those engaged in a bit of smuggling! What better excuse for keeping people away from a certain cave, cottage or wreck where contraband is hidden, than by saying it was haunted!

A classic example of the misuse of the occult way of the sea is probably to be found in the enigma of the *Mary Celeste*. A three-masted barque, the *Mary Celeste*, was built at Parrsborough, Nova Scotia, in 1861 and was owned by the New York shipping company of J. H. Winchester. On November 7 1872, she left New York bound for Genoa and on December 5 was found drifting and deserted some 130 miles off the coast of Portugal by the *Dei Gratia*, which had also left New York, a few days later, bound for Gibraltar.

Books and articles have been written offering solutions to the *Mary Celeste* mystery and the disappearance of her master, crew, passengers and the master's wife and daughter. Solutions range from murder, mutiny and piracy to giant octopuses and water spouts, but scholars now believe that it was a clear case of barratry which was successful because of the general public's belief in the occult way of the sea.

The Ultimate Portent of Evil

From all this, then, we can conclude that the worst omen a sailor could see was a phantom ship. According to sealore should a phantom ship heave in sight, an ordinary mariner could protect himself best by keeping as near as possible to the ship's figurehead (believed to embody the spirit of the vessel and to be literally the life and soul of the ship), or quarterdeck: the quarterdeck being the portion of the upper deck extending from mainmast to stern, the preserve of officers. Nowadays an officer boarding a vessel still salutes the quarterdeck, for in Catholic days a crucifix was hung on the quarterdeck rail; this is an excellent example of how superstitious religious ritual has survived into modern usage.

Even in modern times the sea possesses many mysteries of which sea phantoms are still the strangest. Perhaps the majority of cases of ghostly sightings at sea are mere hallucinations, but many still defy logical explanation: such was the case of the US naval lieutenant whose strange encounter saved the lives of a ship's company and passengers.

During the winter of 1852 the Mexican ship *Chalchihuitlicue* (named after the ancient Aztec goddess of the Jade Petticoat), out of Mazatlan bound for San Diego, was caught in storms off Vizcaino Bay. Conditions were so bad that it was all that the ship's young American captain could do to keep his vessel afloat. Having served as a lieutenant in the US Navy this was the young seaman's first command and it looked like being his last.

The raging sea pounded the *Chalchihuitlicue* mercilessly, and to make matters worse the ship's rudder broke and half the rigging fell, smashing the deck amidships and killing two of the captain's best navigators. The young captain was also knocked senseless by a falling spar. Thus, both crew and passengers seemed doomed to death. Just as the ship was about to be wrecked on the rocky foreshore below San Quintin, however, a strange thing happened. From the bowels of the ship there appeared a man in Mexican naval uniform, who mounted the stairways to the bridge. As if by magic the ship ceased her eccentric course towards the rocks and, rudderless, braved the storm until in the calmer waters of San Diego Bay.

A little before the storm abated the young captain regained consciousness long enough to remember seeing the Mexican naval officer directing the ship's course. He fainted again, however, before he could shout to the stranger. When the captain finally came to, his ship, passengers and crew were out of danger off San Diego roads. In his log, recently found by a research team from the National University of Mexico, the captain recorded his ship's lucky escape, with a footnote on the Mexican naval officer who had appeared from nowhere to guide the ship to safety. The young captain admitted that he did not know who the Mexican officer was, for he had certainly not been on the passenger list, neither was he seen before or after the lucky encounter; yet older sailors among the American seaman's crew knew the stranger well. They identified him as the *Chalchihuitlicue's* first master Captain Porfinio San Luis Madero. What puzzled the young captain most was that Captain Madero had died ten years before!

Selected Bibliography

The following are the main volumes consulted during the research for this book. Other volumes used for subsidiary research are mentioned in the text.

Armstrong, Warren. *Sea Phantoms*, Odhams 1956.

Beckett, Commander. *A Few Naval Customs, Experiences and Traditions*, Gieves, Portsmouth 1931.

Belon, Pierre. *Histoire Naturelle des Poissons*, Paris 1551.

Briggs, K. M. & Tongue, R. L. *Folktales of England*, Routledge & Kegan Paul/University of Chicago 1965.

Brown, Raymond Lamont. *A Book of Superstitions*, David & Charles/Taplinger 1970 & 1971.

Brown, Raymond Lamont. *A Book of Witchcraft*, David & Charles/Taplinger 1971.

Brown, Raymond Lamont. *Sir Walter Scott's Letters on Demonology and Witchcraft*, SR Publishers/Citadel Press 1968.

Cahier & Martin. *Nouveaux Mélanges d'Archéologie*, Paris 1874-77.

Campbell, Commander A. B. *Customs and Traditions of the Royal Navy*, Gale & Polden 1956.

Campbell, J. & Hall, T. *Strange Things*, Routledge & Kegan Paul 1968.

Canning, John (Editor). *50 Great Ghost Stories*, Odhams 1966.

Carmichael, A. *Carmina Gadelica*, Macleod 1900.

Carter, G. G. *The Goodwin Sands*, Constable 1953.

Clair, Colin. *Unnatural History*, Abelard-Schuman 1967.

Croix, Robert de la. *Mysteries of the Pacific*, Muller 1957.

Dampier, William. *Voyages and Descriptions*, John Knapton, London 1729.

Day, James Wentworth. *In Search of Ghosts*, Muller 1969.

De Laval, François. *Voyages*, Paris 1619.

Gesner, Konrad. *Incones Animalium Aquatilium*, Tiguri 1553.

Gibson, J. *Monsters of the Sea*, Nelson 1887.

Gurney, E., Myers, F. W. H., Podmore, F. *Phantasms of the Living*, 2 vols, London 1886.

Hawkins, Thomas. *Book of the great Sea-dragons*, London 1840.

Hole, Christina. *Haunted England*, Batsford 1940.

Hole, Christina (Editor) *Encyclopaedia of Superstitions*, Hutchinson 1961.

Holzer, Hans. *The Lively Ghosts of Ireland*, Wolfe 1967.

Jarvis, T. M., *Accredited Ghost Stories*, Andrews 1823.

Lockhart, J. G. *True Tales of the Sea*, Quality Press 1939.

Macgregor, Alasdair Alpin. *Phantom Footsteps*, Hale 1959.

Macleod, K. *The Celt and the Sea*, London.

Myers, F. W. H. *Human Personality and its Survival of Bodily Death*. 2 vols, Longmans, London 1903.

Oddie, S. Ingleby. *Reminiscences 1912-39*, Hutchinson 1941.

Olaus, Magnus. *Historia de Gentibus Septentrionalibus*, Norway 1567.

Price, Harry. *Short-title Catalogue for the Scientific Investigation of Alleged Abnormal Phenomena*, National Laboratory of Psychic Research 1929. *Supplement* 1935.

Robbins, R. H. *The Encyclopaedia of Witchcraft and Demonology*, Bookplan 1964.

Stow, John. *Annals*, London 1605.

Tirand, H. M. *The Book of the Dead*, SPCK, London 1910.

Toppell, E. *Historie of Foure-footed Beastes*, London 1607.

Tyrrell, G. N. M. *Apparitions*, Duckworth, London 1953.

Index

Numbers in heavy type indicate references to illustrations

A

Abadan   63, 64
ABC   43
Accredited Ghost Stories   122-5
Albert Victor, Prince, Duke of
Clarence   22
Aldrovandi, Ulisse   183
Alldridge, Capt G. M.   130 seqq
Amulets, talismans, charms, etc
                 154, 156, **157,** 158-9, 183
Annals   151
Anne, Queen   47
Ancient Egyptians
         111, 141, 142, **145,** 149, 161-3
Anthelion Phenomenon   43
Antiquitates Donicae   182
Arabian Nights   151
Aristotle   182
Arkansas   183-4
Australia   20, 66, 68
A World Beyond   15

B

Bahamas   116-9
Bahamas Imperial Lighthouse
Service   117
Balfour, Lord   10
Ballyheigue Castle   102 seqq
Barrett, Sir William   13
Beaulieu Abbey   **56,** 101-2
Beaumont, Rear Adm Sir Basil   71
Belfast University   14
Berlingske Aftenavis   68
Bible, The   10-11, 14, 173
Blackwood's Edinburgh Magazine   19
Blake, Adm Robert   135
Blavatsky, Madam H.P.   161
Book of Superstitions, A
                          137, 156, 171
Book of Witchcraft, A
            57, 137, 156, 163, 171
Boston Weekly Newsletter   58
Bozzano, Professor   13
Breacan, Prince, of Lochlarn   96
Britannia   69

British Museum   161 seqq
'Brocken Spectre'   43
Browne, Sir Thomas   171
Bruges   26, 27, 28
Brunel, I. K.   126-8
Buchanan, George   83
Budge, Sir E. A. W.   **111,** 161-3

C

Caesar, Caius Julius   136
California   13
Camden, William   69
Camões, Luis Vaz de   17
Campbell, Shony   125
Canaries, islands   43
Capelle, Adm Eduard von   25 seqq
Carmichael, Alexander   179
Carmina Gadelica   179
Celt and the Sea, The   179
Chatham   71, 99-100, 133
Chile   66, 68
Clanwilliam, Adm Lord   21
Collins, Edward Knight   126
Columbus, Christopher
                       43, 57, 143, 176
Connecticut   42, 43
Cook, Capt James   143
Cornish Feasts and Folk-Lore   97
Cornwall   80 seqq, 121, 150, 174-5
Crawford, Dr W. J.   14
Crookes, Sir William   13
Crosbie, Sir Thomas   104
Cunard, Sir Samuel   126
*Customs and Traditions of the
Royal Navy*   138

D

Daily Express   9
Dampier, William   176
Danish East Asiatic Company
                           66, 67, 103
'Davy Jones's Locker'
(Fiddler's Green, etc)   80, 155
De Bello Gallico   136
De Generatione Animalum   182
Denmark   66 seqq

189

De Rebus Albionicis Britannicus 69
Der fliegende Holländer 18, **33**
Deutsche Werft 62
Diaz, Bartholomeu 17, 143
Doenitz, Adm Karl 24
Doyle, Sir Arthur Conan 14
Drake, Sir Francis 134
Drake's Drum **55,** 134-5
Dunraven, Lord of 88 seqq

E

Eilean Mor, lighthouse **56,** 83 seqq
Emes, Capt J. F. 71
Eratosthenes 142
Essex 99, 150
Eskimos 153-4
Euhemerus 144

F

Falmouth 76
Figureheads **147,** 185
Fitzball, Edward 19
Flannan Isles 83 seqq
Florida 52, 57-8, 117
Fokke, Capt Bernard 19, 20
Folktales of England 172
Ford, Revd Arthur 14-15
Freud, Dr Sigmund 12

G

Gama, Vasco da 143
Gargantua and Pantagruel 182
George IV 137
George V 22
Gesner, K. 183
Gibson, W. W. 86-7
Glamorgan 88 seqq
Godwine, Earl of Essex 70
Good Hope, Cape of 17
Greenaway, Capt James 71
Guardian, The 9

H

Hampshire 101-2
Harris, Joel Chandler 57
Hawaii 61, 63, 65
Hecht, Professor 31
Heine, Heinrich 18-19
Henry, Prince, the Navigator 143
Herodotus 142
Hitler, Adolf 24, 32, 129
Hipparchus 142

Historia Animalum 183
Historia de Gentibus Septentrionalibus 182
Historia Monstrorum 183
Hong Kong **148**
Howard, Lord, of Effingham 70

I

Iliad 149
Invercargill, New Zealand 21
Ireland of the Welcomes 102

J

Jal, Auguste 17
Jamaica 48
James, William 12
Japan 63, **112, 148,** 151-3, 161, 164, **165, 168,** 169, 183
Johnson, Commander 71
Jung, Dr Carl 12

K

Kent 69, 99-100, 106 seqq, 119
King Cnut 70
Kitchener, Field-Marshal Earl **55,** 163
Kristeligt Dagblad 68

L

Lambarde, William 69
Larkin, Professor 13
Legends of the St Lawrence 47
Lincoln, President Abraham 12
Liverpool 59
Lodge, Sir Oliver 9
Lord of the Isles, The 96
Lorelei 83
Los Angeles 49, 61, 62, 64
Lowe Observatory 13

M

Macleod, Kenneth 79
Madrid 43, 57
Magnalia Christi Americana 42
Magnus, Olaus 182
Maine 46
Malaya 160
Mardles from Suffolk 80
Maryland 51, 52
Massachusetts 43, 45, 47, 138, 183
Massinger, Philip 182
Mather, Revd Cotton 42
Medina Sidonia, Duke of 70

Melbourne 20
Memoiren des Herrn von Schnabelewopski 18-19
Merchant of Venice, The 70
Mexico 57, 185, 186
Mirage, sea 15-16, 42-3
Mississippi 47
Montgomery, Ruth 15
Morning Leader 162
Myers, F. W. H. 13

N

Natural History of Norway, The 182
Naval Customs, Expressions and Traditions, A few 138
Nelson, Adm Lord 89, 99, 135, 156
Neptune (Poseidon), and his 'court' 139-40, 144, 149
New Bedford 45
Newbolt, John Henry 135
New Brunswick 41, 46
New England 12, 43 seqq, 183
New Haven 42-3
New Jersey 60
New York 49 seqq, 59, 60
New York State 12
Norfolk 100-1
Northern Lighthouse Board 83 seqq

O

O'Donnell, Elliott 40 seqq
O'Donnell, Capt P. D. 102-4
Odyssey 83
Ohio 184
Os Lusíadas 17

P

Panama 62, 133-4
Pembroke County Gazette 131
Perambulation of Kent 69
Peru 57, 68
Phoenicians 141-2
Pierioni, Professor 13
Pike, James A., Bishop 14
Plymouth 28
Pontoppidan, Erich 182
Portsmouth 76
Poseidon (see: Neptune)
Pythagoras 142

R

Rabelais, François 182
Reed, Capt Simon 73-4
Renegado 182
Ridgeway, T. C., Jr 49 seqq
Rio Cap Line 62
Ross and Cromarty 98

S

San Francisco 22, 24, 40, 174
Scènes de la Vie Maritime 17
Scheer, Admiral Reinhard 25
Schrenck-Notzing, Baron 13-14
Schroeder, Admiral 26 seqq
Schwieger, Kapitänleutnant Walther 25
Scott, Sir Walter 19, 96
Scylla and Charybdis 83
Sea monsters 179, **180-1**, 182-4
Shakespeare, William 70, 136

SHIPS, name of each mentioned in the text:
Abbey S Hart 58 seqq
Acute 134
Affray **53,** 76 seqq
Aid 73
SS Archer 84, 86
Asiatic Prince **35,** 61 seqq
HMS Asp (Fury) 130 seqq
HMS Association 173
HMS Bacchante 21
HMS Barracouta 121-2
Benwood 57
Bremen 130
British Hussar 63-5
Burnus 63, 64
HMS Camperdown 114
City of Eastbourne 63-5
Chalchihuitlicue 185-6
Cleopatra 21
Concordia 174
Copenhagen (Köbenhavn) **35,** 65-8
Curang Medan 60
Daphne 20-1
Dei Gratia 184
Dreadnought 179
Edenbridge 74
Ellen Austin 58 seqq
Empress of Ireland 63

Endeavour 143
Flying Dutchman, 17-24, **33,** 122
Gay Gaspard 45 seqq
General Grant 20-1
Gneisenau 130
Golden Lyon 103-4
Great Eastern **109,** 125-9
Hannah Regan 22-4
HMS Hampshire **111,** 163
Hesperus 84-5
Inconstant 22
Lady Luvibond 73 seqq
La Plata 174
Libera Nos 19-20
Llanstephan Castle 32 seqq, **34**
Ludlow 63, 64
Lusitania 25, **54**
Jamaica 156
Mary 71
Mary Celeste 184-5
Mexico 67-8
Montreal 179
Niagara 63, 64
Northumberland 71-2
Orient 115
Pacific 179
Packet Light 174
Palatine 177-9
Pickhuben 60
HMS Reclaim 78
Restoration 71
Roscius 179
HMS Royal Oak 135
San Joseph y las Animas 57, 58
Scharnhorst **109,** 129-30
Seabird 58 seqq
HMS Severn 121-2
Shrewsbury 70
Silvia Onorato **54,** 75
Skylark (ex-USN Yustaga) 45
Sorrento 70
Squando 40 seqq
Stirling Castle 71
Tennessee 174
The Iron Mountain 47-8
The Wilmington Star 48 seqq
Thresher 44 seqq, **53**
Titanic **110,** 163
Torquay 134

Tourmaline 21
Turmoil 134
U-20 25
U-65 26 seqq, **34**
Ventura 64
Victoria 143
HMS Victoria 114
Victory 156
Violet 72 seqq
Yorktown Clipper 43 seqq

Shovel, Adm Sir Cloudesley
89, 173-4
Somerset 96-7
South Africa 37-8, 66, 68
Spencer, Edmund 182
Stow, John 151
Suffolk 80, 151

T

Tenerife 38
Tempest, The 136
Tillyard, Dr Robin J. 13
Times, The 156
Tokyo 48, 152
Tristan da Cunha 66-8
Tryon, Adm Sir George **92,** 114-5
Twyne, John 69
Tyrrell, G. N. M. 13

U

Union-Castle Line 32 seqq

V

Virginia 50, 52
Visions of the World's Vanity 182
Voyages and Descriptions 176

W

Waghenaar, Lucas J. 70
Wagner, Richard 6, 18
Westlake, Capt James 74
William II, Kaiser 25
William III 137
Wormius, Olaus 182

Y

Yokohama 61, 62, 63, 64, 152
York Minster 122-5

Z

Zollner, Dr 13